The Language Immersion Life

The Language Immersion Life

A GUIDE FOR FAMILIES

Millie Park Mellgren

2017

Copyright © 2017 Millie Park Mellgren

All rights reserved.

ISBN-13: 9781974580255
ISBN-10: 1974580253
Library of Congress Control Number: 2017912888
CreateSpace Independent Publishing Platform
North Charleston, South Carolina

Contents

Foreword to *The Language Immersion Life* ······· vii

Preface: My Language Immersion Life ·········· xi

The Language Immersion Life: An Introduction ··· xv

Chapter 1 Exploring Early Language Learning ············ 1

Chapter 2 Why Choose Language Immersion? ············ 18

Chapter 3 The First Year Experience ·················· 63

Chapter 4 Growing Through the Elementary Grades ······· 82

Chapter 5 The Struggling Learner in an
Immersion Setting ······················· 103

Chapter 6 Homework, Projects and Presentations
How Do I Help? ························· 127

Chapter 7 Active Involvement in Your Child's Experience ··· 143

Chapter 8	The Secondary School Experience: Long-Term Commitment · · · · · · · · · · · · · · · · · 163
Chapter 9	The Language Immersion Afterlife · · · · · · · · · · 191
	Acknowledgements · 207
	Resources · 211
	References · 215

Foreword to
The Language Immersion Life

It was the 1980s. As an experienced language teacher and teacher developer, I had read extensively about immersion education and admired the research results. What I learned about these programs had already begun to influence my thinking and my teaching. Still, full-fledged immersion programs themselves seemed to me to be somewhat elitist and impractical in most school systems. Then everything changed for me, when I received a grant to visit a number of well-known immersion programs, beginning with the original and thoroughly researched French immersion program in St. Lambert, Quebec.

My travels in Canada and the U.S. gave me rich personal experiences with several immersion languages and program models. My visits included extended time in classrooms and conversations with teachers and administrators. I began to understand immersion not so much as a bold experiment suitable for certain settings, but rather as a wonderful learning opportunity appropriate for any interested school system or family.

In those visits I observed many of the elements that make immersion programs so effective, such as:

- Surrounding students with the new language
- Using the new language to teach curriculum content
- Using the new language for real and immediate purposes throughout the day

I saw how these and many other elements of immersion could also make other types of world language programs more effective. I visited and worked with many immersion programs over the years after my memorable introduction, always finding more to admire and more ways to incorporate the insights of immersion to enhance language teaching at every level. By 2017 many of these practices have been widely adopted by language programs and teachers at all levels.

There is one thing that every immersion program model provides, however, that no other model of world language instruction can offer: TIME. Only immersion programs can give learners enough time and intensity in language instruction, through the day and over years, to develop a significant level of fluency. Early world language immersion is an amazing gift for a child and for the adult that child will become.

In *The Language Immersion Life,* Millie Mellgren invites parents to a visit inside the world of immersion, an opportunity in many ways similar to my own eye-opening series of program visits described earlier. She shares her perspective from extensive background and experiences as an immersion parent, teacher, administrator, researcher, and advocate. She brings student experiences to life through the voices of her own children and those of many other young people for whom the gift of immersion has been life-changing. To complete the picture, she includes the voices of other parents, teachers, and administrators, as well.

Mellgren's book provides support and encouragement for all parents considering immersion for their children. The book will also be a trusted companion for those already experiencing *The Language Immersion Life*. Enjoy your visit!

—Carol Ann Dahlberg, Ph.D.
Professor emerita, Department of Education
Concordia College, Moorhead, Minnesota
Co-Author, *Languages and Children: Making the Match*

Preface:
My Language Immersion Life

In 1986, I accepted a position at the University of Minnesota where I was assigned graduate students who assisted in the supervision of student teachers in second languages and cultures. One of these graduate students was Carol Ann (Pesola) Dahlberg, who during the time we worked together was also co-authoring *Languages and Children: Making the Match* with Dr. Helena Curtain, a pivotal work in language immersion education. Dr. Dahlberg heavily influenced my interest in language immersion. I absorbed her passion for early childhood language learning with great enthusiasm. I began working with immersion schools in the Twin Cities through a U.S. Department of Education grant, launching a lifelong enthusiasm for this amazing educational opportunity. I also enrolled my kindergarten-aged son in a local Spanish immersion program. Soon thereafter, I found myself returning to my roots in K-12 education to become an immersion teacher myself.

I had the great fortune years later to work with others in founding the Ada Vista Spanish immersion school in Ada, Michigan, and to become the principal of that school. As principal, I used my experience in language immersion as a researcher, parent, and teacher to inform additional roles as staff development coordinator, program developer, and administrator. Participating in immersion education from this variety of viewpoints has enriched the experience for me many times over. I have known numerous dedicated professionals, and we have shared the joys and challenges of immersion education through our work together. I have worked with thousands of students and parents who traveled this road with me as well. The experiences of all these shared immersion devotees have given life to this project.

In 2007, a large 20th anniversary celebration of the Robbinsdale Spanish Immersion School in the Robbinsdale Area School District in Minnesota was held, providing a rare opportunity to survey language immersion graduates. The Robbinsdale school district offers immersion education for students from kindergarten through 12th grade and these graduates were from the classes of 2000-2007, the first eight graduating classes of the Robbinsdale Spanish Immersion School. Through an online survey, a traditional paper survey, and one-on-one conversations, graduates answered questions about their experiences.

Again in 2016 former language immersion students responded to questions via an online survey. Respondents once again came from the Robbinsdale Spanish Immersion School, as well as from the Forest Hills Public Schools in Ada, Michigan. The Forest Hills students were graduates of the Ada Vista Elementary Spanish Immersion program. Nearly 300 survey responses from these two programs came from students ranging from those who had been out of school for 16 years to others who were in their final years of high school.

In addition to gathering student input, surveys were also sent to language immersion parents and educators in these programs. Responses were also received from language immersion educators in Oregon and Kansas, volunteered by individuals who had heard about the project via connections with the two surveyed programs. Participating parents ranged from those whose children graduated long ago to those who still have students going through immersion programs. Some parents surveyed have grandchildren currently attending immersion schools: the children of their own immersion graduates. Educator responses came from teachers who were new to the profession to those with over 30 years experience in immersion education as well as school administrators. Fifty-seven parent responses were received as well as 21 educator responses. Additional stories have continued to pour in during the writing of this book, as those who live the language immersion life are passionate about their experiences and have many fond memories.

Statements by those who responded from the three survey groups appear throughout this book. Some were willing to be identified and others preferred anonymity. For this reason, quotes are listed with first names and surname initial only, followed by an identification of their role as student, parent, or educator. Where requested by the survey respondent, some names have been omitted entirely, though their commentary remains a valuable contribution to the complete picture. Lest you think survey responses were all female, I should comment that more males asked to be anonymous than females. You will see more female than male names provided after quotes for this reason. Insights from all respondents offer wide perspectives on the Language Immersion Life, whether quoted or included in the narrative. They indicate how passionate parents, educators, and students are about language immersion and its impact on their lives.

My personal experiences have primarily been in Spanish immersion schools and therefore many of the references are related to the Spanish language, though data and stories stem from other language programs as well. The concepts are applicable to all language immersion programs as they produce common issues and successes. Each language has its own cultural and linguistic nuances, but the process of language acquisition for students in these programs is similar, and the results they achieve are equally impressive. Early language learning provides valuable learning input and lasting benefits no matter the language chosen. Whatever language a child may encounter in immersion school, its study will have enormous positive impact. In addition, my personal experiences have been in full immersion programs and traditional elementary foreign language programs. In the following pages these and other options will be discussed. Most examples, quotes, stories and experiences will come from the full immersion model but as with language choice, the process of language acquisition remains similar and though results vary, they remain impressive.

This book uses research and the stories of language immersion families to guide parents as they make choices about immersion programs and to help them navigate programs through high school. *The Language Immersion Life* explores why a passion for language immersion develops, grows and inspires so many. I hope it will instill in you a similar enthusiasm for language learning for children, just as it has for me, and countless others.

– Millie Park Mellgren

The Language Immersion Life:
An Introduction

Sending your child off to school for the first time is an enormously exciting event for parents. You choose backpacks, shoes and clothing, gather school supplies, and prepare for months before the first day arrives. Apprehension grows as you let go of those precious preschool years and release your child into the world of elementary and secondary education. Even if your child previously attended day care programs, there is something unique about that first day of kindergarten—a true rite of passage into school-age childhood.

Whether you wave goodbye as you put your child on the school bus or accompany your child to school on the first day, tears often appear as you flood with emotions over the significance of this event. It becomes difficult to leave your child with the teacher or bus driver, even though you are overwhelmed with pride and excitement that this day has finally arrived. Grandparents, extended family, friends and neighbors also join in the emotions of this important occasion. The kindergarten child senses the excitement and apprehension in the air and begins to acquire these feelings about the first day of school as well.

Like all parents anticipating this milestone, you may have a mix of concern, nervousness, and worry along with your optimism and hopefulness. This stress results from the effort to ensure your child has the best educational experience to shape future opportunities. Options abound for your child, including public and private schools, neighborhood schools, and specialized programs. Among those options flourishes a rich and engaging educational approach known as language immersion. This option presents an exciting and enriching opportunity worth consideration.

A language immersion program includes instruction in what is known as a "target" language. In a Chinese immersion program, the target language is Chinese. A German immersion program has German as the target language, and so on with any of the chosen languages of instruction. Generally, English is considered the "native" language in American immersion schools, although some students who come to schools in English speaking communities speak other languages at home. A dual, or two-way immersion school will have students with English as either the target or the native language. Whether as a native language or a target language, English and at least one other language are developed for each student, and competency is gained in both languages. This book will discuss the attributes of various models of immersion as well as the opportunities, advantages, and challenges of the language immersion life. It is my hope that reading this book will persuade you of the merits of this option and encourage you to seek this setting for your child.

Making the choice to enroll your child in a language immersion program is a tremendous step for your child and the entire family. This learning option will affect you as parents, both older and younger siblings, grandparents and extended family. Indeed, you make a lifestyle choice for your *entire* family, an experience you will share together. Immersion education encompasses the school day, the homework hours, the choice of friends and playmates, the developing interests of the child, and numerous opportunities to interact with other cultures. It is a wonderful lifestyle that enriches the whole family as you face challenges and joys you can only imagine and begin a rich cultural adventure that will bring positive experiences and tremendous growth to your family life.

CHAPTER 1
Exploring Early Language Learning

"My parents figured that learning everything in two languages could only be beneficial in the long run." – Katie Jo J-B, Former Language Immersion Student

"We believed becoming bilingual would create a significant advantage in life for our children." – Language Immersion Parent

Language study began early in the history of our country. French missionaries taught their language to Native Americans as early as 1604 (Simon 1988). We can guess that the French also gained new language skills from Native Americans. Though language study has evolved since those early days, in the United States it is primarily still viewed as a value-added skill, certainly not a requirement for success. In many other countries, however, it is seen as a necessary skill. Canada led the way in initiating language immersion education for children based on the idea that people learn additional languages in the same way they learn their first language—in a natural context where there is social motivation to communicate.

Children have a reputation for being natural language learners, for very good reason. Almost without exception they have learned their native language with apparent ease, and by the time they are 6 years old they have brought it to a level of fluency that is the envy of non-native speakers. Parents who bring their children into a second language setting and immerse them in a new situation—for example, an elementary school taught in the foreign language—often experience a kind of miracle. After around 6 months, their child begins to function successfully in the new setting and at a linguistic level to which the parents cannot hope to aspire, even when they have been studying the language seriously for a similar period of time. (Curtain and Dahlberg 2010)

This ease with language learning was the impetus for wide development of immersion language opportunities for children in Canada ever since their first appearance over 50 years ago. Following closely behind, elementary immersion programs began to develop in the United States, when the Culver City, California school district opened its first language immersion program in 1971. Since that time, immersion programs have shown tremendous expansion throughout North America. The *Directory of Foreign Language Immersion Programs in U.S. Schools* (2011) published by the Center for Applied Linguistics (CAL) documents the growth of immersion schools in the U.S. They note 448 schools, but concede that the data is incomplete as it is self-reported. I am familiar with a number of schools that I could not find in the CAL directory. Others have suggested immersion schools now number in the thousands. The CAL directory is useful, however, in generalizing that the growth in number of schools has more than doubled in the new millennium. In addition, the numbers of students in these programs have multiplied, and now there are new generations in immersion schools, including the children—and even grandchildren—of immersion graduates. Today, former language immersion students are employed in all areas of the workplace and are changing life around them, due to the influence of this type of education on their thinking, their broadened cultural awareness, and their brain development.

Early Childhood Advantage Rationale

> During the first ten or twelve years of life, young children have the mysterious, miraculous ability to learn languages in addition to their mother tongue completely, effortlessly, and to a large extent unconsciously. Because we understand so little about how this miracle occurs, it can fairly be asserted that millions of young children have done this, yet no one can claim to have taught a second language to a little child. (Gaarder 1978)

As awareness of immersion education grows, more parents than ever are seeking to learn why they should start language learning for their children at such an early age, notably kindergarten. Fortunately, research into the language acquisition that occurs in immersion education began shortly after programs opened in Canada in the 1960s and in the United States in the 70s. The findings from these studies still hold true today.

One early immersion researcher, Wallace E. Lambert (1984), noted that most children acquire language effortlessly in the early years of life, making elementary school the obvious choice as the starting point in acquiring a second language. Young children also have less fear of risk taking. They are more likely to attempt to speak, without the fear of what others think, than older teens and adults. Children are more open to the discovery of the world around them, have fewer negative stereotypes, and are more willing to engage in the give-and-take communication that leads to fluency. As Gaarder, who served as a bilingual education expert at the U. S. Department of education for nearly 50 years stated above, we may not understand the miracle, be we can be certain that it occurs.

If you are making the choice of an immersion program for your child, it is important to start as soon as possible, ideally in kindergarten. Many language researchers, as well as advocates for early language learning have long noted rationale for this early start. Krashen's "Monitor Model" assumes that language acquisition is "implicit and subconscious" in the same way a child learns a first language. Attitude is significant. The learner must not only understand the language input but also be open to it (Krashen 1981). Brain "plasticity," or the brain's ability to make connections and form pathways that enable language learning easily, is also important. Many agree that this ability decreases significantly at the onset of adolescence, making elementary school the ideal time for language input to occur.

> Traditionally, there are three classes of theories as to why there is a rapid loss of language learning ability with age; a precipitous loss of the neurological flexibility to learn a language (e.g., the permanent entrenchment of cerebral asymmetries in the brain); a "filling up" of the language-learning capacity simply due to the experience with the first language; and the superposition of an intellectualized self-conscious way of learning everything, which interferes with the elementary language learning process. (Krashen 1981)

Another advantage children have is that their young age allows them an early start. They simply have more educational time ahead to master all they possibly can of traditional school content in both the target and the native language. Gladys Lipton, a major proponent of languages in the elementary schools and author of *Elementary Foreign Language Programs* (1998), also notes that children are curious creatures and that the strange sounds of languages, as well as the customs of other countries, are all items that spark natural curiosity. She adds that children are excellent mimics, who don't mind the repetition that allows them to develop good habits of listening and correct pronunciation. Tapping this natural learning interest of children not only gives them more time to learn but also utilizes those very language-learning skills that are most eagerly displayed by the very young.

When I first became enthusiastic about early language learning, my husband was somewhat amused by my comments about the amazing learning skills of young children. I had visited schools and witnessed children speaking two languages and was very impressed by the successes I saw. Of course, I was comparing these children to my former students in high school and university second language classes. The elementary school kids were using the second language so much more freely. I lauded the skills of teachers who brought children to such competent levels in a second language.

My husband's perspective came from his experience working for the United Nations, assigned to a post in Lesotho, Africa. He recalls very young children from all parts of the world who lived in the United Nations housing compound. Many were too young to attend school but spoke multiple languages quite easily. It was common to hear children playing in the yard, moving in and out of multiple languages as they interacted with different people. Their parents did not speak languages as easily, so young boys and girls were frequently called upon to be interpreters in this international community. Opportunity, exposure, and necessity were the drivers of instruction for these children. This was a natural language immersion experience.

Social, Cultural and Global Rationale

Over 25 years ago, Senator Paul Simon in his important book *The Tongue-Tied American,* shared significant anecdotal information regarding the lack of language skills in the United States compared to other countries around the world. Senator Simon notes, "Because of this language gap the loss to the nation's cultural life is inestimable. We are linguistically malnourished. Yet never in history has there been one nation with such a variety of ethnic and language backgrounds." He supports these statements with numerous examples demonstrating how the lack of language skills has hurt the country in terms of trade, security, employment and education. Simon notes, "It is essential for United States security to maintain communication with people everywhere. To the extent that we ignore an unknown nation and an unknown people, to that extent we ultimately risk our own security." In 1958 President Eisenhower sent a special message to Congress stating, "The American people generally are deficient in foreign languages, particularly those of the emerging nations in Asia, Africa and the Near East. It is important to our national security that such deficiencies be promptly overcome" (Simon 1988).

In recent years, numerous publications have noted continuing concerns related to the lack of second language proficiency. A simple computer search will reveal a wide variety of sources noting that the problem Senator Simon spoke of years ago sadly remains today. *Education Week* provided commentary on this issue, noting, "American graduates may be technically competent but are increasingly culturally deprived and linguistically illiterate compared with graduates from other countries competing for the same jobs" (Jackson, Kolb and Wilson 2011). The journal notes that 20 of 25 industrialized countries start teaching world languages in grades K-5, and 21 European countries require nine years of language study. This solidifies the argument for American students to develop the linguistic and cultural skills that are part of the core curriculum in every other part of the world. "It is high time that Americans were no longer bound by their linguistic limits"(Jackson, Kolb and Wilson 2011).

Though limited exposure to languages has long been a concern, there are many who do recognize today the importance of language learning and cultural understanding. Gail McGinn, retired Senior Language Authority in the Department of Defense notes, "Understanding foreign cultures and regions is important, but adding foreign language to that understanding provides a decided edge critical to global security in all of its aspects, from war fighting to assisting developing countries, to combating disease" (McGinn 2015). Numerous offices of the federal government recognize the importance of languages to the future of the country including the Department of Defense, the Office of Management and Budget, the State Department, the Federal Bureau of Investigation, the Central Intelligence Agency, the Center for Disease Control, the Department of Education and the Department of Labor, among others. Nearly all have issued reports or promoted initiatives related to language learning and cultural understanding. Nancy McEldowney, recent Director of the Foreign Service Institute stated,

> One of the most crucial aspects of diplomacy is the ability to get inside other peoples' heads, to know what they think, how they think, and why they do so. Our diplomats must be thoroughly fluent, not just in foreign languages but also in the issues that matter most to those we're dealing with . . . This type of advanced regional, substantive, and linguistic expertise is acquired not in weeks or months, but rather over years of sustained and focused effort (2015).

Leon Panetta, former Director of the CIA, has noted as well,

> Language is the window through which we come to know other peoples and cultures. Mastery of a second language allows you to capture the nuances that are essential to true understanding . . . This is not about learning something that is helpful or simply nice to have. It is crucial to CIA's mission (CIA Press Release 2010).

In 2014, Congress asked the American Academy of Arts and Sciences to study the nation's current capacity of knowledge of languages and follow with recommendations "to ensure excellence in all languages as well as international education and research." The Academy, founded in 1780 by statesmen and business leaders, included John Adams, Samuel Adams, John Hancock and James Bowdoin. These early members believed that appreciating the "plurality of languages would improve communication domestically and internationally." Nearly 240 years later, the report of the Academy's Commission on Language Learning summarizes their findings stating,

> While English continues to be the lingua franca for world trade and diplomacy, there is an emerging consensus among leaders in business and politics, teachers, scientists, and community members that proficiency in English is not sufficient to meet the nation's needs in a shrinking world, nor the needs of individual citizens who interact with other peoples and cultures more than at any other time in human history. (American Academy of Arts and Sciences 2017)

The report also notes that while 66% of European adults have knowledge of more than one language, only about 20% of adults in the United States report this knowledge, indicating that we, as a nation, "risk being left out of any conversation that does not take place in English." With this great lack of people with skill in additional languages, many are missing out on business and employment opportunities. There are increasing numbers of businesses operating internationally, and multilingual employees are highly sought after and valued.

While 20% of adults report *knowledge* of more than one language, less than one percent of Americans are *fluent* in a foreign language and only 7% of college students are enrolled in a foreign language course (Friedman 2015). While elementary language study had a slight surge in the mid-90's to slightly over 30% of schools, that number had dropped to around 25% by 2008 (Pufahl and Rhodes 2011). Given this data, the Commission on Language Learning concludes that the ultimate goal of any effort to improve language learning should be "improved access to language education for all U.S. citizens, irrespective of geography, ethnicity, or socioeconomic background" (2017).

Gladys Lipton sums up the value of early language learning:

> Students are made to realize the importance of other ways of doing things. This may well be one of the best ways to teach the new generation not to discriminate against, belittle, or be unwilling to accept people simply because they are 'foreign.' If students have not had exposure to, or appreciation of, foreign languages and lifestyles, or do not understand that people can be different, they will have no understanding, respect, or interest in foreign concerns and people. (1998)

Helping children attain global skills and understanding through early language learning may be one of the most important things we can do as parents and educators to promote peace and goodwill on the planet. Many of the parents who have supported immersion schools in the past are those with international experiences who immediately grasped the importance of language immersion for their children's futures. Fortunately, there are a variety of elementary school models and approaches to help us in reaching this lofty goal.

> *"In addition to their gift of language my children have a greater sense of the world globally and historically. I see how the world 'makes sense' to them. If they were not in the immersion program the world would not have been as accessible to them as it is now."*
> *– Catherine C-H, Language Immersion Parent*

> *"My kids simply view the world much differently than their non-immersion peers. They are much less entitled and much more tolerant of differences."* *– Krista F, Language Immersion Parent*

Early Language Learning Models

In what I believe is the most important book written on language education in the elementary school, *Languages and Children—Making the Match*, Drs. Curtain and Dahlberg (2010) list twelve key concepts for success in elementary and middle school language learning. This list contains guidelines for classroom application of research that can be utilized by teachers and administrators in early language programs. From those concepts, a few key points for parents to look for in a setting where children learn languages best are:

- Students are actually using the target language and teachers are instructing with minimal use of the native language.
- Lessons focus on themes and show balance of academics, culture, and language.
- Students become increasingly independent in their use of spoken and written language.

- Students learn grammar through use of the language, not analysis, and there are frequent, meaningful opportunities for language use including storytelling, music, games, rituals, drama, celebrations, and other hands-on experiences.
- Activities are interesting, engaging, culturally connected, and take into account distinctive levels of educational development and a variety of learning styles.
- Reading and writing are communicative tools appropriate to learner age and interests.

Most quality elementary language programs, regardless of the model employed, will include these elements. They are key to what you should look for in an early language opportunity for your child.

I recall one of my first visits to an elementary language program, accompanied by the Minnesota State Foreign Language Supervisor, Suzanne Jebe. We enjoyed a pleasant observation in the classroom where the teacher delivered instruction to her students completely in the target language. I was impressed. As we were leaving, the students lined up at the water fountain in the hall for drinks. The teacher joined the students in the hall and immediately began monitoring their behavior, telling them to "Line up!" "Keep your voices down!" and "Quickly! Only take a drink for a count of 3!" These instructions were all in English. It didn't strike me as unusual since we were outside the classroom until Suzanne leaned over and said words I have never forgotten, "What are the students learning about which language *really* is the most important for communication?"

This simple question changed the way I looked at language programs for the rest of my career. With one simple question, I learned how linguistic values are imparted to students and how communication is truly taught. From that point forward, I have always looked not only at classroom lessons, but the entire educational setting as a contributor to language learning.

Take time to visit a variety of programs and models if you have several options from which to choose. Look for active, engaged students. Listen to be sure you hear the target language, if not exclusively, frequently and meaningfully. Observe the core values of the program with regard to language, culture, and academics. You know what your child enjoys. Look for *that*, only presented in a language other than your child's native language. If you find happy, engaged students—and you are mostly hearing the target language—you are on the right track to finding an immersion home.

Non-Immersion Program Options

In your search for an early language learning opportunity you may encounter programs described as FLES (Foreign Language in the Elementary School). These programs typically have special pull-out classes similar to the way Art, Music, and Physical Education are taught at the elementary level. Depending on the program, the teacher may use the target language exclusively, part of the time, or very little of the time. A wide variety exists within this model depending on curriculum used and program goals established.

Another model is FLEX (Foreign Language Exploratory), one that uses class instructional time to learn *about* languages, with classes taught mostly in English. These classes sometimes include samplings of a variety of languages. These classes rarely have competence in the language as a primary goal but rather focus on exposing students to language study and what might be gained from learning another language. FLEX classes may stimulate interest in future language study but generally do not provide a solid foundation for further language learning.

Both models, especially FLES, contribute to early language learning in areas where immersion models are not feasible or accepted, particularly if they follow the concepts for success as outlined by Curtain and Dahlberg. I personally believe that any exposure to language learning at an early age is beneficial, and all program designs contribute at least somewhat to the goal of global and cultural learning, no matter the model. However if you desire more of that early language exposure, you will need to look at an option with greater time spent in the target language.

The Language Immersion Option

> *"Immersion is a phenomenal program that allows children to learn another language without even realizing they are learning it."*
> – *Former Language Immersion Student*

Language Immersion is an educational approach in which the standard school curriculum is taught in the target language. From the first day of class, teachers speak to students in the target language and avoid English at all times. Students learn the language easily and begin comprehending what the teacher is trying to communicate almost immediately. Even after decades working with language immersion programs, I still feel my scalp tingle with excitement as I witness students in their first week of school following directions given by their teacher in a new language. The ease with which children acquire language is always a thrill to observe.

In Language Immersion four main goals are addressed:

1) Students will achieve mastery of the regular elementary school curriculum.
2) Students will acquire proficiency and skill in the target language.
3) Students will acquire the same proficiency and skill in English as students in an English-only program.
4) Students will gain global and cultural awareness and understanding.

While the wording of these goals may vary slightly from program to program, these are the foundations upon which immersion programs are developed, and they reflect the outcomes desired for all students. Lambert (1984) has noted that immersion teachers take students to a level of functional bilingualism that could not be duplicated in any way other than living in and attending school in a foreign setting. Students achieve target language competence without suffering loss of native language skill development, without falling behind in school content, and without mental confusion or loss of normal cognitive growth. Immersion program goals are indeed lofty and courageous, but also completely achievable, as the growing body of research data continues to validate. As a parent, you most likely want it all—a successful student who learns everything school has to offer while maintaining their native language and gaining competence in a second language. Is it too much to ask? Generations of language immersion graduates are living proof that reaching these goals is indeed possible.

> *"My parents' primary goal was to have me succeed in school so I could go on to live a better life than they currently had or would ever have. Placing me in an immersion program was the first step in achieving that goal." – Cecelia R., Former Language Immersion Student*

> *"I am very grateful to have had the language immersion experience. The process of learning a second language at a very young age is so much more effective than trying to learn it later in life. It was very valuable to be exposed to another language and other cultures from a young age. It opened doors for me and I am very thankful for that." – Former Language Immersion Student*

In a language immersion program, learning activities occur in the target language. "Immersion is easily able to provide a holistic language learning experience for students of a new language, since the teachers and students are able to communicate throughout the entire school day on topics spanning the full range of the curriculum" (Curtain and Dahlberg 2010). However, a variety of language immersion models exist with varying amounts of time and academic content included in the target language instruction.

You most likely will not be able to choose the model unless you live in an area where there are many schools offering various types of programs employing different immersion instructional models. Unless you are involved in the pioneer stages of program development, you probably will accept the local model with gratitude that any program whatsoever is available to you and your family. Either way, it is important to be aware of the various models and their expectations. You too may wish to be a pioneer and pressure your district for the program model of your choice. Parents can be powerful forces for educational change, particularly those who come with an understanding of the options available and have solid rationales supporting their requests.

The original model in North America is known as *full immersion*. Typically, the students in these programs are native English speakers and receive all instruction in the target language for the first two years, learning to read first in the target language. English language arts is added in second grade for approximately 30 minutes each day, with time added each year until English time may increase to nearly 50% of the day in grades 5 or 6. A variation of this model begins English instruction in first grade rather than waiting for second grade, while other programs wait until third grade to begin English instruction. The advantage of waiting until at least second grade is that students *learn to read* in a single language first. After developing reading skills in the target language, the transfer to English, generally the student's home language, goes very smoothly and quickly. By delaying English instruction, the target language is more firmly rooted and forms a solid base for all learning to occur throughout the school years.

My personal preference is to delay English instruction until second grade. However, I have worked in programs where English instruction starts in first grade and those where English is introduced in second grade and find that students thrive in either model. I have no personal experience in a program delaying English until third grade, but the rationale behind this decision is understandable and could be an effective programmatic decision as well.

A second model is *partial immersion,* where a lesser amount of time is spent in the target language, often around 50% of the school day or one or two subject areas. Reading is generally taught in both languages in this model. At least one other subject area is usually taught in the target language in addition to language arts. A district often chooses this model due to challenges in staffing a program. While a partial immersion program will not achieve the results of a full immersion program, it still operates from the same basic goals and students receive better results than no immersion experience whatsoever. In addition, students receive language and cultural exposure at an early age, opening brain pathways for future language learning.

A third model is called *dual or two-way immersion,* a program that has gained popularity in the new millennium. Children are placed in mixed classrooms of English speakers and native speakers of the target language, with the goal of both language groups becoming bilingual and academically successful in both languages. This model generally adopts either a 90-10% or 50-50% design for time spent in the target language and English. Language arts is usually the prime content area taught in dual immersion programs, along with at least one other subject area, often math or social studies. An advantage of the dual immersion program is the inclusion of students from both language cultures, providing peer input in addition to teacher instruction when learning the language of the other group. It is a very powerful tool for motivation and learning when students have the opportunity to teach each other. In addition, mixing students from both language backgrounds contributes to rich cross-cultural understanding and friendship.

Whichever model you choose or have available to you, all programs offer the opportunity for your child to be exposed to a second language at the critical early age needed for optimal language learning. Regardless of the model, it is preferable to spend as much time in the target language as possible because more time spent engaged with the language leads to greater language acquisition. On the other hand, any and all exposure to a second language is input that will enhance your child's life. Your child will experience the gains of cultural awareness, the brain development that accompanies language learning, and a valuable lifetime skill no matter which model of elementary second language learning you are fortunate enough to access.

"Learning another language was amazing! They can kind of understand French and Italian now as well. When traveling to Spanish speaking countries, their language skills have helped them immensely. Their cultural awareness increased and made them more well rounded people." – Diana S, Language Immersion Parent

CHAPTER 2
Why Choose Language Immersion?

"I think attending an immersion elementary is the single thing that has most shaped my life's path." – Ellen T, Former Language Immersion Student

"Immersion couldn't have changed my life more. I wouldn't be anywhere near the same person I am today if it weren't for the program." – Former Language Immersion Student

Why would anyone *not* choose language immersion? Obviously there are far more English-only programs than immersion programs. Therefore, the majority of the population either does not know about language immersion, does not have access to a program, or chooses not to participate in this tremendous opportunity. Along with mastery of the four main goals of immersion education introduced in Chapter 1, an immersion program offers gains in general academic competence, brain development, and social and personal skills. This leads to the development of a wonderfully well-rounded student, ready to take on the world after graduation.

As a principal, each year at kindergarten parent information meetings, I would discuss these goals and explain how each contributes to the overall richness of the language immersion experience, and why parents might choose this option for their families.

Sharing my convictions regarding this educational lifestyle was one of the joys of my career. This chapter, in essence, is your introduction to the meeting we called Kindergarten Roundup, where I explain the four main areas that students are expected to master.

- The regular elementary school curriculum
- Proficiency and skill in the target language
- Proficiency and skill in English comparable to students in an English-only program.
- Global and cultural awareness and understanding.

Goal 1: The School Curriculum

Your child will learn everything in the language immersion program that is taught in every other elementary building in your school district or in other neighboring schools. Successful mastery of the regular elementary curriculum has always been evident in immersion schools. Your kindergarten student will acquire early reading and math skills. Social Studies, science and health concepts will be covered as well as any other topics also presented by neighboring schools. Now, with more clearly defined state and national standards for education, you can be sure that any accredited program is following this educational plan. In other words, the curriculum designed by your state will be followed; however, students will learn the content in their immersion language. You can have a great deal of confidence if this is a public school, as it is subjected to rigorous review by the state each year.

With a non-public school, you need to do a bit more research yourself to ensure it is meeting state and national standards, whether you opt for an immersion program or any other traditional program. For the most part, this information, in the form of student test scores, school ratings, or success reports, is readily available on the school website or on the state education department website.

Most private schools follow the standard state curriculum, and you can be confident your child will receive the knowledge and skills needed for post-secondary education. Again, you should research any program to satisfy your questions about curriculum.

With language immersion, students not only master the elementary curriculum, but a wealth of research on immersion has consistently shown that students either do as well as students in other schools in the district, or more commonly, outperform students in English-only programs in the same district. This is a profound finding from over 40 years of studies in immersion programs.

The earliest studies of French immersion programs in Canada have noted that students perform at a level equal to or higher than their peers in English-only programs (Lambert and MacNamara 1969). These results have been replicated year after year since the mid 1970s by the Culver City Spanish Immersion Program and across the United States in numerous other immersion programs. For example, Lindholm-Leary (2011), who has researched language development in children for decades, reports study results to support this finding in Chinese two-way immersion programs, suggesting consistency across both languages and program models. Additional studies by Lindholm-Leary also find similar results across socioeconomic backgrounds (2011, 2014, 2015, 2016a, 2016b).

Standardized academic testing given in most schools, usually beginning in third grade, is almost always done in English. Even though language immersion students learn the concepts in a target language other than English, they consistently outperform students in English-only programs on district, state, and independent assessments, which require them to demonstrate their knowledge in English.

Because my goal is to give families a general overview of immersion education and its benefits using the first-hand accounts of students, parents and educators, this book does not attempt to offer a complete review of the results of research on language immersion. That information is readily available in a plethora of articles, found on the Internet or through libraries and professional organizations, and especially from resources listed at the end of this book. Research has been astonishingly consistent in documenting the positive outcomes of immersion education and I do share many pivotal studies in these pages. If you have further questions regarding immersion research, I encourage you to investigate the wide body of information available.

Goal 2: Proficiency and Skill in the Target Language

"Anytime anyone asks where I learned my Spanish, I don't stop bragging about immersion. Multiple times people have asked where I'm from, assuming I grew up in a Spanish-speaking country." – Hannah C, Former Language Immersion Student

The main reason parents enroll their children in an immersion program is the desire for them to learn a second language. The words "opportunity to learn another language" or a variation on those words is always given by new immersion education parents when discussing their rationale for considering this program.

"To learn to read, write, listen to and speak a second language— well." – Language Immersion Parent

"Americans are so far behind the rest of the world in learning a second language. I wanted my kids to be bilingual (I didn't even care what language!) to give them an advantage over their peers when looking for a job. I also believed that learning a second language increases the brain to learn other things (math, music, etc.) I knew starting young was the key to fluency." – Krista F, Language Immersion Parent

Few elementary school parents have concerns about target language proficiency in the early language grades, though sometimes parents become concerned in middle school or high school when their kids need to switch from general fluency to grammar-based or academic language skills. However, even though students may need grammar "tune-ups" at this point (just as they would with English language skills) you can be confident that your child will be successful in reaching a much higher level of target language competence than students who do not begin in an early immersion program.

Fifth through eighth grade students in dual-language immersion programs overwhelmingly express confidence that they have target language skills to give and get information as needed, express opinions, understand and interpret the target language on various topics in both written and spoken forms, and present ideas and information to others on a variety of topics. Comparative teacher ratings of their students' skills equated very closely to the students' ratings of their own skills (Lindholm-Leary 2016a). The results from dual-language immersion students align closely with the confidence in target language skills expressed by students in full immersion programs as well. Parents surveyed by language immersion educator Hillary (2007) shared the following observations about their children's target language skills:

My children:

- Speak Spanish with native Spanish-speaking children outside of school.
- Receive compliments on their accents as they speak with native speakers.
- Enjoy hearing people speaking Spanish in public and understand them.

- Are not afraid to speak in Spanish.
- Can communicate with native Spanish speakers at the Latin Festival.
- Can help their high school siblings with Spanish.
- Can write to relatives that speak Spanish fluently.
- Want to learn another language now.

Whether parents, teachers, or the students themselves rate target language skills, all participants are generally satisfied with the immersion language learning experience and have confidence in the students' ability to use the language in settings both within and outside of school. Students at the secondary level rarely achieve this result with such confidence.

"Immersion instilled in me a passion for learning since the very beginning....I was exposed to such amazing things at a young age....I can definitely tell a huge difference in college also. I have a knack for Spanish that non-Immersion students just don't have. The material comes easier to me and I am a natural and confident speaker." – Former Language Immersion Student

"I feel like there's more for me out there now that I have this knowledge and background. I feel like I can communicate with more people and be able to relate to them." – Skylar S, Former Language Immersion Student

Students gain competence in the target language and in the use of languages in general, including their native language, as they grow. They will draw on this skill throughout their educational experience and as they move into social and employment settings as adults. Even those who never or rarely use their target language find that the language background is often useful.

> *"Despite my years of using Spanish on a very infrequent basis, I never completely lost the ability to understand or speak it, and can still read and write in Spanish fairly well."* – Cecelia R, Former Language Immersion Student

> *"I traveled to Mexico this winter and spoke fluently even though I hadn't spoken Spanish in years."* – Kelsey W, Former Language Immersion Student

Goal 3: Proficiency and Skill in English

In most programs, kindergarten is taught fully in the target language. English instruction begins sometimes in first grade, but more commonly in second grade on a limited basis, with time spent in English increasing each year through the elementary grades. School personnel aim to ensure that students are functionally competent in both languages as they progress through their educational experience. Functional competence refers to the ability to communicate and complete tasks in a language. Proficiency in speaking, listening, reading and writing are all expected and developed. This is generally measured by having immersion students complete the same assessments as English-only students, using their English, not their target language skills.

The main academic concern for parents is the fear that their child will not excel in English—the language they will need when they move on to post-secondary education. Even though I was an educator working with language immersion programs, my husband had these concerns for our own children as they entered elementary school. He valued language and culture education and had several experiences of his own with world language learning, but he still wanted assurance that our children would be prepared to do college-level work in English. This hesitancy appears often in families: one parent really wants the early language option for the child and the other parent or another relative has concerns about

English instruction and future English skills. Sometimes one parent is sold on the importance of language learning in general and the other parent simply doesn't see the need for it, believing that English is enough to succeed in today's world.

The former senator from Illinois, Paul Simon, points out errors in thinking, "if English was good enough for our Founding Fathers, it's good enough for me." He notes that some of the Founding Fathers did not speak English, and of those who did like Jefferson, Franklin and Adams—many also spoke other languages and found this ability useful in their work. Simon's humorous commentary: "The Founding Fathers did not have automobiles, airplanes, sewer systems, electricity, and a host of other things we find of value, but I would not want to abandon these conveniences because of the lack of historical example" (Simon 1988).

You may not need convincing that simply mastering English is insufficient today. However, I have seen many cases where either one parent is not convinced of the urgency to start their five-year-old learning a second language, or there is pressure from extended family or friends to "drop this crazy talk" about learning a second language. The pressure from others to focus on English first may be so intense that you begin to have doubts about placing your child in this type of program, even though you are convinced of the value of being bilingual.

> *"The only problems that I still see to this day with English is I sometimes try to pronounce English words as if they were Spanish words. It results in some interesting interactions." – Cecelia R, Former Language Immersion Student*

> *"I did not have fears about English. My main goal for my children's education was that my children enjoyed education since it would be such a huge part of their lives. All three of them loved immersion and made lifelong friends. My children have excellent English." – Sandra B-S, Language Immersion Parent*

I assure you that your child will develop English skills thoroughly and competently in a second language immersion program. To begin with, remember that your child lives in an English environment. Though 6-7 hours a day are spent in the target language setting, English speaking children wake each morning and end each evening with loved ones who are speaking English. When English is not the language spoken at home, children still watch TV and go to sports, classes, clubs, and other activities primarily conducted in English. In restaurants, stores, parks, museums, and nearly all other surroundings, your child is exposed to the English language. English vocabulary will continue to increase just as it does for children in English-only programs. In school, though students learn standard elementary curriculum in the target language, the brain is able to process that input and learning occurs in both languages. What a miraculous wonder our brains are!

Though students, teachers and researchers have all noted initial lags in English, principally in spelling, in the early grades, this early delay is made up quickly, often as early as third grade, and students go on to be successful in their English classes throughout their educational experience. Fifth to eighth grade students in dual-language immersion programs, as reported by Lindholm-Leary (2016a), indicate overwhelmingly (92%) that they can read and write well in English for their grade level, and perceive they have sufficient English skills to understand their written class materials and engage in classroom interaction. Dr. Lindholm-Leary's research results consistently demonstrate that students develop oral and literate proficiency in both English and the target language as compared to their English-only peers, despite differences in ethnic or racial groups, socio-economic levels and language minority groups (2014, 2015, 2016a, 2016b).

Additional data presented from four different language immersion schools in the Twin Cities of Minnesota show higher scores in reading, math and writing, all on tests conducted in English, when compared with their school districts and other comparison schools with similar populations. These four districts included the very highest socio-economic suburban areas, middle range socio-economic neighborhoods, as well as schools in the urban districts of Minneapolis and St. Paul (Downs-Reid 2000). Language immersion does not diminish English language skills even when students receive either half, or most, of their instruction in the target language in the elementary years.

Analysis of data from the Ada Vista Spanish Immersion School near Grand Rapids, Michigan, revealed equal or higher scores in both reading and math by third grade students. Higher scores were noted in reading vocabulary, total reading, math concepts and applications, and total math areas of the California Test of Basic Skills (CTBS), a test administered in English. Researcher and immersion administrator Hibbeln (2004) notes, "Clearly if a parent wants their child to become bilingual at an early age, they can feel confident in enrolling their child in an early immersion program without sacrificing any achievement in their native English."

Similar results were noted very early in the language learning process of grades 1-3 French immersion students. Students were tested for literacy skills in both English and French and made comparable gains in both languages. Researchers noted that, "French immersion does not impede English language and literacy skill development" (Au-Yeung, et al. 2015). French immersion students also demonstrated successful performance on English-language proficiency tasks, in spite of their education being conducted in French, in research conducted by Bialystok, Peets, and Moreno (2014). Also, in an Italian two-way elementary immersion program, students achieved moderate-to-advanced levels of writing proficiency in both Italian and English by the upper grades, an important component of language competence (Montanari, Simón-Cereijido, and Hartel, 2016)

Compelling research from the Portland Public Schools was conducted over a four-year period, with programs in both dual immersion and one-way immersion programs, and in both Mandarin Chinese and Spanish immersion settings. Reading ability for young students was measured in months, for example a student reading at the beginning of the year in fifth grade would be at the 5.0 level and if on track in December, four months later, would be reading at the 5.4 level. This research found that students outperformed their peers by seven months of English reading growth in fifth grade and by nine months of English reading growth in eighth grade, which means they were nearly a full school year ahead in reading compared to non-immersion eighth grade students (American Councils for International Education 2016). These are powerful results that provide evidence that this approach leads to greater educational achievement.

The research supporting successful curricular, target language, and English competence goes on and on. I have presented but a sampling of the many studies that have intrigued practitioners and researchers over the decades that language immersion has grown in North America. Results are varied, as in any school system, but immersion has revealed itself to be effective at helping children meet the regular school curriculum goals in English, all while being taught in a second language.

As an example of what immersion students one day will be able to do, note that they should be ready to write college essays in both languages by the time they graduate from high school. In reality, though, they will acquire many of the needed skills to do this much, much earlier. Their skills in listening, speaking and reading will most likely be even stronger than their writing skills. This is generally true in both the target language as well as English.

"English and writing have never been my strong subjects. I think I've done fairly well though." – Former Language Immersion Student

"I was afraid that I would have a lower competency in English writing, but my fears were unfounded." – Emily P, Former Language Immersion Student

Goal 4: Global and Cultural Awareness

After language acquisition, the reason most stated by parents for choosing language immersion is "global perspective." Parents today recognize the importance of this knowledge to their child's future. Sometimes the child has been adopted from the target language culture and parents want to provide a heritage experience that they themselves cannot provide. Other times parents simply desire for their child to be immersed in a cross-cultural setting. Students in language immersion programs learn to accept and understand global cultures in general and the target culture quite fully. This is actually one of the strongest outcomes of an immersion program. Achieving this goal alone is an excellent reason to choose language immersion, and is one of the biggest life-changers for immersion students. Graduates often confirm how being immersion students altered the path their lives had taken.

In an address given at the 25th anniversary of the Robbinsdale, Minnesota Spanish immersion school, immersion graduate Maria Blonigan Cisneros (2007), stated:

"Our parents put us in this program because they wanted us to learn another language. I'm here to tell you, it's not about the language. It's about who we've become, what we've learned to be, what we have studied, whom we have married. We make choices now because of who we have become, because of language immersion."

What language immersion teacher, administrator, or parent would not have a sense of doing the right thing, and of making a contribution to the future of our planet through the development of broad-minded individuals such as Maria? I am so proud of the accomplishments of every immersion graduate I have met, and I agree with Maria's statement that graduates from immersion programs have made choices in life that were determined by the global and cultural education they received. The language is a bonus skill! Nearly all parents who stated that they chose language immersion for "the opportunity to learn a second language," later on emphasize that the outcome of this choice is so much larger.

> *"Aside from being bilingual, which is such an awesome thing to see happen as a parent, cultural and global awareness are areas I underestimated. My daughter seems so much more worldly than her peers in traditional schools. She has an appreciation and a curiosity about the world around her that I don't see being taught at the traditional schools." – Michelle C, Language Immersion Parent*

Sarah Jerome, former president of the American Association of School Administrators stated,

> We must create schools where learning about the world and learning to live in harmony are basic lessons for all children.... All our efforts are driven by the common goal of developing future generations of truly global citizens. We are working for a better world—not for ourselves, but for all the world's children and their children's children. (2007)

Parents of former immersion students are now realizing that they made the choice of language immersion not only for their children, but also for their grandchildren. They now are watching their grandchildren being raised bilingually from birth by their immersion graduate children. The Language Immersion Life becomes a choice that transcends generations into the future, as well as being a choice for your family today. Parents often do not recognize how different their children are becoming until the high school years when they view their children alongside new non-immersion peers. Only then do students and parents recognize how immersion education has influenced their growth as a family linguistically and culturally.

Changes in the behavior of immersion families were noted in the early 1970s in Culver City, California. Parents reported beginning or resuming their own study of the language. Families planned food menus, travel experiences and special events in order to expose their children to the target culture. They watched Spanish language television, purchased Spanish books and magazines, and socialized more with Spanish-speaking neighbors and acquaintances (Campbell, 1984). You might find that your family engages in this type of cultural adventure once you embark on the language immersion journey. Your contributions to the cultural development of your child will grow at home as your common interest in both the target and other global cultures grows.

Yong Zhao, New Foundation Professor at the University of Kansas, has called for American education to add foreign languages and cultures, and advocate global citizenship for all. He states,

> To ensure a better society for all, actually to ensure the very survival and continuity of the human civilization, requires us to prepare our students to become global citizens. As such, students need to be aware of the global nature of societal issues, to care about people in distant places, to

understand the nature of global economic integration, to appreciate the interconnectedness and interdependence of peoples, to respect and protect cultural diversity, to fight for social justice for all and to protect planet Earth, home for all human beings (2008).

In Zhao's book *Catching Up or Leading the Way* (2009a), he lays out three challenges for education in a global world:

- We must help our children secure jobs that will provide for them and their families.
- We must help our children live, work, and interact with people from different cultures and countries.
- We must help our children adopt a global view in their thinking and to develop a sense of global citizenship.

These challenges demand much of parents and educators. However, they must be inherent in the education provided to raise responsible children and future leaders.

Language Immersion education is the perfect home for cultural and global skills to flourish, through the basic curriculum and by exposure to other cultures. Every immersion school I have worked with or visited is a fabulous example of the type of cultural instruction called for in education.

> *"It definitely made me realize at a young age that the world is a big place, that I am privileged/lucky, that people are different and that's ok!" – Former Language Immersion Student*

> *"Learning a language significantly impacts your ability to be aware of other people and cultures. Languages are windows to the world and having two languages means I have two opportunities to assist the world through the lens of others. I am*

passionate about cultural and social awareness and my immersion education is at the root of that." – Janet G-M, Former Language Immersion Student

Language immersion offers the bonus of cross-cultural interactive skills that will be useful in any profession your child undertakes. Again, Mr. Zhao (2008) notes,

> "The ability to interact effectively with people who speak different languages, believe in different religions and hold different values has become essential for all workers. That is, what used to be required of a small group of individuals—diplomats, translators, cross-cultural communication consultants or international tour guides—has become necessary for all professions."

Dual-language immersion students perceive that they have a better understanding of target language people than their peers who are not in immersion. These also agree that learning the target language helps them understand more about speakers of their immersion language and that the readings and topics they have studied help them understand target culture people as well (Lindholm-Leary 2016a).

> *"Knowing another language opens up not only that culture, but it removes the fear people often feel about trying something new or meeting someone unlike themselves. I can't imagine my life without the people I've met and places I've been. I attribute that 100% to my bilingual education, my exceptional teachers, and my parents."* – Former Language Immersion Student

I am thankful every day that my husband and I chose language immersion for our own children. As adults they have found that these immersion skills are indeed useful in their current professions.

As a high school teacher, one son works with Spanish speaking students, parents and colleagues and feels fortunate to be able to communicate with them in their home language. The many global experiences gained in immersion education also assists in understanding students and families from many cultures within his school population. My other son, as an environmental attorney, also finds the cultural and global skills useful as he travels the country working with different groups of people, preparing his legal cases. He needs to relate to various communities and finds the ability to listen with respect and understanding, regardless of cultural background, were developed long ago in the immersion program (and hopefully at home as well).

The global future is here now, and each succeeding generation of students will increasingly need the solid background in global education and cultural sensitivity that is gained naturally in an immersion program.

"In addition to the ability to speak and comprehend Spanish like a native, immersion gave me a greater awareness of different cultures. It planted a seed for global awareness and interest that expanded beyond those countries and cultures where Spanish (my immersion language) is spoken." – John M, Former Language Immersion Student

"I am convinced that these kids… are more open to the world, understand cultural influences and nuances and appreciate the perspective of other people far more easily…(Our daughter) is completely open to new experiences, viewing food and property and money differently and understands happiness means different things to different people. That insightfulness, particularly at such a young age, I do not believe would have happened had she not participated in an immersion learning experience." – Marla B, Language Immersion Parent

Language educators have long noted the importance of cultural education within the curriculum, but now it is being recognized that global awareness must be integral to the curriculum and can no longer be seen as a "luxury item" (Wilberscheid 2005). Language immersion education provides this experience, integrating cultural and global awareness fully into everyday learning. Diversity is not just a topic to be covered; it is a natural outcome of the greater understanding that comes from immersion in another culture and language through literature studied in class, books in the library, art and maps on the walls, and many other materials found in classrooms and other areas of the school building. In addition, singing and listening to music, watching movies, cooking food, making flags, learning about customs usually are included in the immersion experience, providing extensive cultural enrichment. You may find that your language immersion child begins to integrate this cultural knowledge into the daily life of your family.

> *"The other day, on a long car trip, my children took control of the music. For two hours, we listened to the top 50 songs in Spain, mostly in Spanish. They were both able to sing along with all the songs. When we arrived at our destination, I asked, 'Did you do that just so you didn't have to listen to me sing along with the radio this time?' It was true—I'm a terrible singer." – Lisa M, Language Immersion Parent*

Each of the teaching teams I worked with introduced food from whichever culture we happened to be studying at the time. We taught children that they should taste everything as part of their cultural immersion process. Students were encouraged to give it a try with the caveat that they could not say, "Ick" or "Yuck" or "That's gross!" We taught them acceptable responses such as, "Es diferente" or "Es interesante." It was always interesting to later hear them use those expressions when discussing a new dish in the school lunchroom. Global education and cultural study experiences such as these surround students in immersion classrooms, giving them an added bonus in their education and hopefully leading them to greater cultural awareness.

Parents have told me years after the student was in my class that their child still loves going to art museums and other cultural institutions, a skill gained when in language immersion school. One student let me know that he still seeks out beautiful Spanish art, has loved the art of Joan Miró since fifth grade, and has it hanging in his living room even now. A small thing? Possibly. I believe it is indicative of gaining cultural appreciation from an early age.

> *"Global and cultural awareness are huge. The ability to talk to and connect with people who are different than me keeps me grounded and in touch with the world. It's also just nice to speak another language and have access to diverse music, movies, articles, etc."*
> *– Maria C, Former Language Immersion Student*

> *"Immersion gave me a deeper appreciation for cultural nuances and diversity from a much younger age than my non-immersion peers. The importance of this perspective cannot be understated in our increasingly globalized society and workforce." – Former Language Immersion Student*

A favorite quote, displayed on my office wall, is from Genelle Morain who once taught at the University of Georgia. She was approached by a school board member who asked, "Why should a student who will never leave Macon, Georgia study a foreign language?" Her simple but wise response: "That's *why* he should study another language!" (quoted in Simon 1988). As one who grew up in small town Kansas, I couldn't agree more. I am so thankful my school offered both Spanish and Russian, and I had the opportunity to study both. Though I lived on the wide, open expanses of the Kansas prairie, I learned to dream about far away places and what life there might be like. I became interested in people of other backgrounds and cultures, even though I experienced no diversity of culture in my school until I left for college. Exposure to a second language has influenced my life ever since, providing direction to what I studied, who I developed friendships and relationships with, and eventually determining the framework for my marriage and career. I've seen this same influence on the lives of thousands of my students and their families as well.

> *"Immersion allowed me to travel places and understand what people there are saying. I am more aware of how other cultures function because of the things we learned in immersion. I had more opportunities because I spoke Spanish, which I think made me a better person." – Former Language Immersion Student*

> *"Each of our three Spanish immersion children developed deep desires to further explore language and culture. Now in high school and college, they have explored French, German and Japanese languages, respectively. In addition, they are interested in the cultures of others with no hesitation in befriending students of extremely different backgrounds. In fact, our children seem to crave culture in a very healthy manner." – Kathleen P, Language Immersion Parent and Educator*

Academic Competence and Brain Development

Academic challenge, brain development, creativity, and rigor are also top reasons given by parents for choosing immersion education. Some parents arrive at the immersion school because they are looking for something to offer a challenge to their child. Either the child has been highly successful in preschool, has started reading, or displays early academic development in several ways. For a wide variety of reasons, parents want a challenging environment for their budding academic.

> *"I was always mature for my age. My parents purposely put me in immersion education because they thought I would be bored with a 'typical' educational setting."* – Anita M, Former Language Immersion Student

> *"It provided an excellent opportunity for them to be challenged. My oldest needed a school that would engage her more than a traditional elementary. Learning a language kept her from being bored."* – Krisanthy S, Language Immersion Parent

> *"Challenge and rigor. My son had mastered the kindergarten curriculum already and it was recommended that this program would offer him the rigor he needed."* – Language Immersion Parent

I have often told incoming parents that brain development is indeed a strong reason for choosing language immersion. While parents of students who are advanced may feel this is a unique opportunity to challenge their child, the advantages in brain development are evident in all learners. For those seeking a challenging setting however, immersion education provides many opportunities. There is often less boredom noted in the classroom for high potential students, possibly due to the newness of everything in the immersion environment, or possibly because adding the layer of language over traditional learning creates additional challenges that keep a young brain engaged. In addition, teachers are used to thinking creatively to present information in a second language and therefore are prepared for students who also think creatively as well.

> *"Immersion challenged their brains to learn in a more sophisticated way."* – Beth D, Language Immersion Parent

Some say that learning a second language can make you smarter, improving cognitive skills across the board. It seems that a second language forces the brain to strengthen itself by resolving internal conflict, giving the mind a workout, so to speak. The brain has to stay focused, switch attention from one thing to another, and perform mentally demanding tasks (Bhattacharjee 2012). Students in immersion schools unknowingly switch languages in their mind quite often, relating what is happening in the target language to what they have previously learned in their native language. They monitor the environment around them, sort through the input of the classroom, and make sense of it when combining it with what they already know. "The bilingual child has had to decipher much more language input than the monolingual child who has been exposed to only one language system. Thus, the bilingual child has had considerably more practice in analyzing meanings than the monolingual child" (Cummins 2000). They are more flexible thinkers. When students are already engaged in a high degree of deciphering and analysis, teachers can use strategies to enhance cognitive ability further.

Immersion teacher Olberg states, "Immersion teachers use a variety of methodologies to teach academic content areas. You get more bang for your buck." It is true that the variety of teaching strategies used to make content understood in a second language by young children happen to be effective for ensuring that content sticks in those sponge-like brains as well. This may offer a partial explanation for why children do so well learning content, even though it is taught in a second language, or it may simply be the extra processing the brain goes through to file away information. Whatever happens, it is a wonderful process that is a marvel to witness.

> *"Learning another language allows the child to tap into one more part of their brain that normally wouldn't get used. It is exercise for the brain."* – Kristi H, Language Immersion Educator

> *"Being immersed in two languages helps a student's ability to problem solve. The brain develops numerous pathways (connections) that allow a child to analyze information in different ways."*
> – Language Immersion Educator

> *"Greatest impact was having to learn EVERYTHING in Spanish at a young age. It forced them to use their brain differently and I truly believe that this is why they both excel at school. They understand their environment around them better. They can see culture happening and have an appreciation for it. And this also draws the families in so that we, too, were a part of that process." – Krisanthy S, Language Immersion Parent*

In a study of 788 fifth to eighth graders who were enrolled in either a Spanish-English or a Mandarin-English immersion program, students indicated that they can think about information across languages, translate from one language to another, and can think in different or more creative ways. They also noted more confidence in their ability to do well in school due to their bilingualism (Lindholm-Leary 2016a). These student perceptions about their own positive cognition skills are powerful and remind me of the statement, "What you think about, you bring about." Interestingly, some research has even found positive influences in cognitive development after only three years in a language immersion school experience (Nicolay and Poncelet 2012). While I encourage parents to make a long-term commitment to the language immersion life, it is reassuring to know that even shorter term exposure to this educational opportunity will reap benefits for young children.

> *"I feel my immersion education pushed me to think in different ways and to attempt to understand things from different perspectives. I feel it prepared me to persevere through challenges and to explain my thinking in a variety of different ways." – Allison M, Language Immersion Educator and Former Student*

> *"I think he became a more well-rounded individual. I also feel it helped his brain development and made it easier for him with all of his studies, especially learning languages." – Shawn W, Language Immersion Parent*

"The language skills they are learning will help them get past obstacles in life because they have to be willing to persevere when things don't make sense. I think that knowing a second language helps them problem solve." – Language Immersion Parent

In my survey of immersion school graduates in Minnesota and Michigan during the first decade of the new millennium over 83% had GPAs of 3.0 or higher in high school and nearly 52% had GPAs of 3.6 to 4.0. The national average GPA as reported in *The Nation's Report Card: America's Graduates,* during the same years as the graduations of my respondents, ranged from 2.94 to 3.0 (Nord, et al 2011). Immersion survey respondents were therefore over the national average 83% of the time, and significantly over the national average more than half of the time. These are solid results and definite assurance that immersion education prepares students to be college ready. Studies reviewing ACT and SAT scores of language immersion students also reveal positive results: immersion students generally rank higher than their peers.

So while your concerns right now are about your child's success in kindergarten, you should be aware that many of the benefits of studying a language in the early years stay with your child throughout their lifetime and most certainly through their academic years.

"I think learning two languages has helped build their neuron network, along with helping them with their math comprehension. They are confident learners and I think as they go out into the world they will see what a gift it is to have learned a second language." – Language Immersion Parent

"I think that the study of language had a huge impact on my children. It's simply good for the brain! It connects with music and math and other language skills…all good. My children absolutely did better at other academic skills because of the language program they were immersed in." – Anne J, Language Immersion Parent

> *"Our daughter's class had 40 valedictorians and salutatorians at the two high schools. Most of these high achieving students were from the immersion program. I believe it was a definite factor in developing their other academic skills." – Jan L, Language Immersion Parent*

A study conducted in an urban school district in the western United States compared dual-language immersion students to students in four other elementary schools. The dual-language immersion students scored significantly higher in both math and science (Tran, et al. 2015). In addition, dual-language immersion students in the Portland Public Schools received higher achievement scores in science, math and reading as compared to non dual-language immersion students (Steele, et al. 2013). Even if your dream is for your child to become an engineer, a mathematician, or a rocket scientist—and yes, I really know an immersion graduate rocket scientist—or some other non-language-centric field, you should give this opportunity every consideration.

Language learning helps the brain develop in a way that makes young students more successful in all academic areas as they continue through adolescence and beyond. Researchers at Northwestern University note that a biological difference in the auditory nervous system appears to enhance attention and working memory among those who speak more than one language. "You are a mental juggler," notes Dr. Nina Kraus, professor of neurobiology and physiology at Northwestern. This research also notes that people who can master more than one language are building a more resilient brain, one more proficient at multitasking, setting priorities, and perhaps, better able to withstand the ravages of age" (*Wall Street Journal*, 2012).

Ask any language immersion teacher and they will tell you the benefits: brain pathway development, improved focus, improved decision making, cognitive development, increased analytical skill and improved memory. This list alone should provide sufficient reasons over and above the obvious benefits of language and cultural understanding to choose language immersion. But wait, there's more!

Social and Interpersonal Skills

Another benefit of language immersion is the basic multilingual exposure that has been determined to facilitate interpersonal understanding. Students who are learning to accept others who are different from themselves start to form a close-knit community. The immersion setting then becomes a haven of acceptance for high and low achieving students alike. Research has shown that children in multilingual environments learn very early the importance of adopting another's perspective for communication thus gaining basic skills in interpersonal understanding (Kinzler, 2016). Talk about vital job skills! I would choose immersion for my child based on those essential skills alone.

Students often comment that the ability to use their language skills with others and have native speakers respond enthusiastically encourages them to interact even more in a variety of local or distant settings. This gives them even more confidence in their ability to learn. In my role as school principal, I frequently had parents visit my office to tell stories of their children using their language skills in the dentist office, at a store checkout line, or on a family vacation. The pride of parents is only surpassed by the excitement shown by students as they become braver and more confident in their language abilities.

> *"It has impacted the entire course of my life. I am more culturally competent and socially aware than many people who don't have this educational background." – Former Language Immersion Student*

> *"I think I learned to be more independent from an early age because my parents could not help me."* – Hannah C, Former Language Immersion Student

> *"Being able to converse with a wide range of people has been a really large boost in confidence."* – Former Language Immersion Student

Another of the remarkable social skills of immersion students is their uncanny ability with humor, often in two languages. Humor is a high-level skill in the language-learning continuum; one that is not usually attained except by highly advanced speakers. Humor involves nuances of language including multiple meanings of words, plays on words, and unusual manipulations of words—tasks that require higher-level language skills. Many immersion teachers would agree that they note humor quite early in their students' language development. I don't know if this is an outgrowth of immersion in developing the "cleverness" center of their brains or if immersion kids are just smart-alecks, but they are wonderful creators of humor. They definitely love a good joke and also using their language skills to play jokes on others. Humor is but one of the many social skills possibly developed at a richer level via a language immersion experience. I have no empirical data to support my humor premise, only years of observation by myself and other colleagues. I challenge language immersion researchers to do follow-up research on this idea because I believe it to be true.

> *"I won't lie to you. I use (Spanish) to eavesdrop on random conversations and make Spanish pun jokes. Occasionally I try to impress a girl."* – Former Language Immersion Student

> *"The look on someone's face when they can't figure out how this gringo is speaking Spanish like this is priceless."* – Former Language Immersion Student

"If it weren't for language immersion, I would be a terrible dancer."
– Former Language Immersion Student

As noted in the above section on brain development, language immersion also appears to boost creativity. It might be proposed that the years of creating with language, putting words and sentences together in a language that is not native, may boost the creativity center in the brain as well. While amplified creativity helps students in the academic arena, it also helps them develop social and interpersonal skills both inside and outside the classroom. As one student wrote:

"Learning a second language is a fantastic skill set and necessary in today's world but it's the other aspects that I learned in conjunction with the language that have truly shaped me as a person. The experience taught me how to be creative, to think outside the box and relate to people from different cultures." – Cecelia R., Former Language Immersion Student

Actually, many students have referred to "thinking outside the box" as an outcome they received from their immersion education. As students mix in with English-only students later in the course of their education, or as adults in the workplace, they recognize that by comparison they have great creative thinking and problem-solving skills that stand out to themselves as well as others.

"15 years later and my parents still don't know more than two words in Spanish so I think the language barrier really made me learn to problem solve on my own from a young age." – Hannah C, Former Language Immersion Student

"I feel my immersion education pushed me to think in different ways, and to attempt to understand things from different perspectives. I feel it prepared me to persevere through challenges

> *and to explain my thinking in a variety of different ways."*
> *—Former Language Immersion Student*
>
> *"I feel I am more accepting and willing to try new things and experience new cultures as opposed to some of my friends who did not have those same opportunities." – Former Language Immersion Student*
>
> *"Language and argumentation were skills I developed. My memory skills and logic increased dramatically due to the extra language. I definitely grew into a more cultured, more competent person overall than if I had only learned English." – Emily P, Former Language Immersion Student*
>
> *"The immersion program has enhanced my life and helped me to become more well-rounded." – Former Language Immersion Student*

Senator Paul Simon (1988) also had wisdom to share about social and interpersonal aspects of language learning in terms of self-enriching experiences:

> We learn both little things and big things through the nuances of language. We smile and laugh and cry at our mistakes and those of others. And when we learn another language we catch those subtleties that cannot be transferred. How do you explain *gemütlich* to someone who does not speak German? The simple pleasure you receive from being able to communicate, to visit another country and be able to buy your railroad tickets, or ask questions about a menu, or ask directions—these are self-enriching experiences. Foreign language knowledge also brings an appreciation of music, reading, cooking, gardening, dance and movies."

The self-enriching experiences noted by Senator Simon are part of that social and interpersonal skill base that becomes part of the student's life. New ways of thinking about oneself, as well as others, stem from the immersion experience. "It expands your worldview, so that you not only know more, you know *differently*" (Fortune 2012). The aspect of "knowing differently" is evident to all who come into contact with immersion students. As an administrator, I often gave tours of the school to visiting officials and dignitaries. They usually expressed amazement upon departing, not only for the powerful language skills they witnessed, but also the students' demonstration of self-confidence and concern for the perspectives of others. Visitors would almost always be astounded by our students' knowledge of the world as well, often showing depth of understanding and social maturity not seen in much older students and even some adults.

Early studies of Canadian students note that immersion students perceived themselves to be more like French Canadians who are bilingual than did students in English programs. In writing about "Why I like being Canadian," immersion students wrote with a broader perspective, commented on the varied cultural and linguistic composition of their country, and noted the possibility to speak more than one language in Canada much more often than the monolingual comparison students (Swain 1984). This is a mature type of social awareness I have often noted among immersion students.

> *I find that immersion kids tend to think differently, more out-of-the-box, and are more goal-oriented than others. Where our peers are still struggling with themselves, we seem to have a stronger sense of who we are, where we're going, what our skills are, etc. It's incredible!"* – Emily P, Former Language Immersion Student

Career Opportunities

College and career advantages, job opportunities, better job prospects, and advantages over peers when looking for a job are also rationales put forth by parents influencing their decisions to enroll their child in an immersion program. The data gathered from hundreds of former immersion students would indicate that these parental wishes have been fulfilled. Students have shared numerous stories about the opportunities they have encountered due to their immersion education. As an employer, even outside the immersion setting, I look for people with cross-cultural experiences on their résumés, and I am convinced that many others do as well. Often businesses do not formally require foreign language competence, but more rapid advancement and greater opportunities abound for those with language skills.

A report by NBC News noted numerous job postings that were aimed at bilingual workers who were in demand for both low and high-skilled positions. Marco López, a marketing agency executive vice president, told NBC News that being bilingual "is an extra added value that you (bring) to the table." Also interviewed in this news report, Nicole Houser, an associate dean at Saint Peter's University, included, "Students are stronger cognitively when they learn multiple languages, and that translates to any workplace environment. If you understand multiple languages and multiple cultures, it makes you more marketable" (Cusido 2017). In Chapter 9, many former immersion students will share information about how immersion impacted their career choices and opportunities they have encountered post-immersion. Here is one former student summing up her experience in language immersion:

> *"I believe that I am a totally different person than I would have been if I had gone into an English-only program. Immersion education*

gave me a love for other languages and cultures, connected me with people I may have never met without knowing Spanish, caused me to think more globally and critically, and opened doors for travel, further education, and careers that I would not have had if I had not been a part of an immersion program." – Allison M, Former Language Immersion Student

Children of Native Speakers

Many native speakers also choose language immersion for their children. This may seem unnecessary to monolinguals and even to some native speakers. However, it is a great choice for children of native speakers, as well as children of English-only parents. The goals of the program are equally valid for both sets of students: to gain competency in both English and the target language, to develop cultural and global awareness and sensitivity, and to master the elementary curriculum. Some immersion parents have listed "maintaining cultural heritage and native language" among their top reasons for choosing immersion.

Another group of children who fit the category of "children of native speakers" are those who have been adopted from a country where the target language is spoken. These children have experienced varying degrees of input from the native language and culture, depending on how old they were when adopted. Parents of adopted children often wish for them to learn more about their heritage culture at an immersion school because they do not have the skills or experience to provide this opportunity at home.

"My children were of Latin American heritage. I wanted them to become fluent in Spanish for cultural reasons. Our children were adopted from Colombia as infants so this was a 'no-brainer' as far as we were concerned." – Language Immersion Parent

Even if a child has learned to speak the target language at home with one or both parents, chances are that these parents still want their child to become an "educated native speaker" of the language. I have known parents who did not put their children in an immersion school thinking, "Oh, we will just continue to speak the language at home and they'll be fine." Sometimes this works out well, particularly if the parents are heavily committed to their child's education in the target language. However, I have seen immersion program students gain opportunities over a child from a native-speaking family when they get to high school, college or the employment stage simply because the native-speaking child cannot formally read or write well in the language. Parents do not always pass on the formal skills students learn in school without devoting a great deal of time toward this cause.

> *"My husband is a native speaker of Spanish, but he doesn't speak Spanish with the kids. Sometimes I worried that immersion teachers would expect more from my kids given their family situation. However as years passed and I talked to teachers I learned that our situation wasn't as unique as I had thought." – Jennifer H, Language Immersion Parent*

> *"The incredible pride they feel for both heritage language and culture is invaluable. They are not only bi-lingual but also bi-cultural and bi-literate, reading and writing at a high level in both English and Spanish. They view the world as a very open, interesting and beautiful place. They both have a high interest in travel and learning not only about Spanish speaking cultures, but ALL cultures."*
> *– Language Immersion Parent*

A child's devotion to parents and their willingness to speak the language of the parent is strong in the preschool and early elementary stage. With time, however, the influence of peers wins out over parents, and children often refuse to speak their parents' language. (I know, can you believe that? Those darned peers.) An immersion program takes advantage of peer pressure. Children continue their interest in the language partially due to family history, but also because it's what their friends are doing as well.

Like the parent of any child, a native speaker of the target language is also making a decision that affects the child not only now in kindergarten, but also for a lifetime. If you want your native-speaking child to be competitive in the job market where the target language skill might be a plus, or if you just want to maintain competence in the heritage language so it can pass on to your grandchildren, consider a formal language immersion education as a way to amplify the wealth of opportunities available.

Two Common Questions

Parents often ask me, "Which language should I choose?" It is a good question for which there is no perfect answer. I believe what is important is choosing language immersion itself. Obviously, if there is a family history connection, a community connection, or any other personal reason that drives your language choice, follow that instinct. If not, it is simply important to tap into the brain development and plasticity of the young child; the language choice is not really that important. We can't look into the future and know if our children will need to know Chinese, Japanese, Spanish, Arabic, or Norwegian. We can only provide the opportunity to learn a language, develop the cultural and global understanding, and hope their developing brain will gain the capacity to learn more languages easily in the future. You may only have the choice of one language in your school district. Whatever language it is, go for it! Don't hesitate just because it is not your first language choice. Choose immersion education.

The other question I am often asked is, "How should the school be staffed?" Again, this is a good question without a perfect answer. Should all teachers be native speakers? Should the principal be a native speaker? What about other school staff?

Let's start with the most impactful person your child will see every day, the classroom teacher. Elementary immersion teachers are regular elementary certified teachers who happen to also have great language skills. For my own children, of course, I wanted it all—the best language skills *and* the best teaching skills. What was most important to me was that my child had a caring teacher who understood education well—good classroom management, excellent teaching strategies and a solid knowledge of educational practices. I considered it a bonus when a teacher had fabulous language skills based on a quality cultural experience such as study abroad or other travel around the globe, whether or not they were a native speaker. As a principal, I looked for the same qualities I looked for as a parent. It was important to screen for excellent target language skills, and finding native speaking teachers from a wide variety of backgrounds was a bonus, but good teaching skills were paramount. So the answer is no, a teacher does not have to be a native speaker. On the other hand, with all other things being equal, having language skills at the level of a native speaker is desirable. Unfortunately, schools can't always find enough native speakers or teachers with near-native language skills to staff their programs. Usually, the longer a school exists, the more native speakers they are able to attract. This results in the percentage of native speaking teaching staff growing along with the school.

The administrator of an immersion program is obviously another critical component of a quality school. I have been a teacher in programs with both native speaking and non-native speaking principals. While a native speaker adds a cultural dimension and authentic speaking voice that gives depth and richness to a program, these are not the only skills needed for successful administration. I believe a top priority is that an administrator know, and can repeat, the immersion research inside and out. They must be able to answer quickly the questions that parents bring to the conversation.

Two quality administrators I worked for were not native speakers and had not even studied languages themselves. Sure, sometimes they made comments about language learning that caused teachers to roll their eyes, but those two principals could cite immersion research with the best and hold their own in any discussion of immersion strategies. I also worked with a native speaking principal who knew quite a bit about immersion and also brought her cultural background into the setting.

Many other principals I have known come from a wide variety of backgrounds with varying degrees of effectiveness. So, my answer would be to not judge an administrator based upon certain pre-conceived qualities and instead get to know them and make your own assessments. They all bring a unique set of skills to the immersion setting. Obviously, they should also have general administrative skills such as the ability to manage the building, inspire the teaching staff, and work effectively with students and parents. As a parent, you want your child to be in an inspiring and safe environment where those who work with your child are both effective and caring. You want an administrator who can build that environment. Target language competence is truly a bonus on top of all the other skills and knowledge the administrator must possess.

Other staff in the building may or may not be native speakers. Often custodians, cooks, special education staff, and instructors of special classes like art, music and physical education, among others do not have language skills. Many programs strive to have as many of these positions staffed by speakers of the language as possible. Be grateful for any staff that do have language skills but do not expect that your school will be 100% target language speakers. Most programs endeavor to hire instructional aides that are native speakers to augment teachers in the classroom. This practice is a real bonus to the program and enriches your child through contact with people from a range of cultural backgrounds.

Getting Into A Program

Hopefully by now you are noting the benefits of language immersion and are thinking about enrolling your child in a program. You need to do your research on the program. Attend parent meetings. Talk with teachers, administrators and current parents. Visit the school. Observe classes. Ask questions. The evidence is there for you to gather if the school has been open for at least a few years and the "pioneers" have done their work.

I would not be doing the process justice if I did not warn you that just because you decide you want to be in a language immersion program means you can just walk in and sign up. Many programs, if they've been open for a few years, have limited space available. While it may be possible to easily gain acceptance in your local program, I personally have not worked with a program that did not have a waiting list. For example, the Seattle Public Schools Hamilton International Middle School, which features an immersion continuation program, had a 250-student waiting list on opening day (Schachter 2011). In Jenison, Michigan, parents lined up outside the school on a Sunday, in order to camp out all night, so they could be some of the first to register in the Spanish immersion program the following morning (WOOD TV 2017). In Portland, Oregon parents also wait in line to enroll their children. Many move to Portland, and specific neighborhoods, just to be able to get into the immersion program (Sykes, Forrest, and Carpenter 2016). All the immersion programs I have worked with have had parents moving into the district and trying as many strategies as possible to beat the lottery system and get their children enrolled. I recall receiving a surprising call from a local hospital where a mother had just delivered her baby. She wanted to know what she needed to do to get him enrolled in the program. Yes, immersion parents are a special group of engaged and assertive people.

Remember that immersion programs generally only accept students in kindergarten, although some accept first grade admissions as well. After that time, because a student hasn't learned to read first in the target language, it is very difficult to gain entry. Placing your child's name on a waiting list is an important first step because immersion schools usually have far more applicants than openings available. In this case, each district will have its own policy for entry. Many have a lottery that is purely random. Portland Public Schools has a multi-tiered policy that takes into account neighborhoods, heritage language background, siblings, Head Start enrollment, and income levels. This policy works toward achieving a balanced student population (Sykes, Forrest, and Carpenter 2016). Others have formulas where they take certain percentages of students from in-district versus out-of-district populations. This is how my older son gained entry into the immersion program, through one of the reserved slots for out-of-district students. Sometimes districts take students who live not only within the district, but also in the school's neighborhood boundaries first, and then fill remaining slots with students from other in-district schools.

Most districts also have a sibling policy, granting automatic admission to any siblings of students already in the program. This is a great policy because the language immersion life is truly a lifestyle for the whole family. Allowing families to have all their children in one school makes life easier for everyone. My younger son gained admission to immersion under the sibling policy. Sometimes there is a "children of immersion staff" policy granting first admission slots to children of people who work in the building. This is beneficial not only to these staff families, but also for all families with children in the school. If your child's teachers can reduce distractions and stress by having their own children attend the same school, this makes the immersion experience better for all. In addition, if the children of program staff also attend the school, teachers are even more invested in the program and its success.

So, you can see where this is headed. If your district has 100 openings and siblings fill 30%, another 10% taken by staff families, and another percentage go to out-of-district families; the pool for your child to gain admittance has greatly diminished. Become informed about the entry policies; get on the list as early as allowed. Stay in the communication loop to be aware of any admission developments, including Facebook pages, listservs, and any other information channels offered by the school district. Submit all required documentation. In our district, if parents did not submit required paperwork, we would give those slots to students on the waiting list, even if admissions were closed. Also be aware that some families will apply and gain admission and then have a change of plans, thus opening up last-minute slots.

Even though the information schools share with the pioneer parents in the early years of a program's existence is the same information shared with new parents years later, competitiveness to get into the program seems to grow each year. This may be a result of a growing population of parents sharing information directly, encouraging others to follow the same path, and therefore increasing the program's value to all. A program with an established reputation, which has parents out spreading the word, is one that is coveted. It gets competitive, so make your decision as early as possible and do what it takes to gain admission. If your child is not admitted, stay connected and see if opportunities open up midyear or even the following year. Each program has its own policies and it is worth your while to study them and learn what you can do as a parent to be a part of this opportunity.

> *"Having our children become bilingual was extremely important to us. We feel so fortunate that we 'won the lottery' and they were able to receive this opportunity."* – Jennifer H, Language Immersion Parent

Yes, Language Immersion is a GREAT choice for your child

For over 30 years I have described language immersion as "the best gift" you will ever give your child. I still believe this is true. I have watched thousands of children in immersion programs grow into competent, caring adults who possess not only additional job skills through their proficiency in two languages but also global understanding. They are indeed different adults than they would have been otherwise because their parents chose this educational option for them.

> *"I find it to be one of the best things that my parents gave me, an opportunity of a lifetime. I constantly see how attending an immersion school has opened doors for me that otherwise would have never existed."* – Erica S, Former Language Immersion Student

> *"This program is the greatest gift anyone could receive.... Every day that passes I grow more and more grateful for this fantastic experience and would love to share it with my family in the future. The immersion program taught me things I couldn't have learned anywhere else and gave me opportunities I will cherish for the rest of my life and for that I thank anyone involved."*
> – Former Language Immersion Student

Besides being a gift, language immersion is also an adventure. You have to trust that this method of learning will provide positive benefits without knowing exactly what that outcome will look like in

10-15 years. You place your family life on the line by choosing this lifestyle—the language immersion life. As a parent, only you can make this choice for your child. It is *you* who will determine that an immersion experience will be valuable for your child, and the kindergarten year is the correct time to give that gift. As noted earlier, after kindergarten it is very difficult to gain entry into an immersion school unless the student has grade level skills in the target language, so the time you invest prior to kindergarten to learn about this option is critical.

> *"The whole experience for our family was wonderful. The language immersion school was a 'jewel' in the public school system. We always felt like our kids had the benefit of a private school education. The teachers and administrators were fantastic. We loved them all. Their attitude and dedication were awe-inspiring. It had great impact on our children, nothing like they would have received in an English-only program." – Barb N-M, Language Immersion Parent*

> *"Immersion is mental gymnastics. We've been lucky to travel several times as a family. Watching my kids talk in Spanish to everyone has been amazing. They get directions for us, take tours in Spanish and explain what is going on. They feel so comfortable in another culture. Immersion has been an unbelievable blessing!" – Julie C, Language Immersion Parent*

Though you may be convinced that this is the best educational opportunity for your child, you may hear resistance from extended family and friends, thereby delaying your decision and the resulting application process. Without seeing the results of immersion, others in your circle may not be convinced and may try to dissuade you or at least let you know they think you're crazy. Take the time to educate your detractors a bit, but also realize that you are the one who has done the research, visited the schools, and observed in classrooms. Don't let others delay your action or your child could miss out. You can always start the process by applying to programs and then worry about debating your decision later.

Be strong in your resolve. You know your child. You know your goals. You have discovered the path that can lead your child to successful competence in two languages and in multiple cultures. You do not necessarily need to convince others to buy into your decision. Just take the first steps on that path and let your friends and family observe the results. In the end, you'll be the wise one, and they'll wish they had discovered immersion first.

"I believe my extended family was very supportive of my parents' decision, but probably didn't understand it or think it was necessary. My parents thought differently." – Cecelia R, Former Language Immersion Student

My husband and I chose the gift of language immersion for our family nearly 30 years ago though most family and friends did not understand what we were doing. Years later, they see the positive results. I am immensely proud of my own two children who went through immersion programs and are now making notable contributions to the world. Both have used their Spanish skills repeatedly in work and social settings. In addition, I cannot overestimate the value of cultural and global exposure at an early age in forming who they are now as adults.

Stories from immersion students and their parents continue to reinforce the value of immersion education for me, even though I have long been passionate about this educational model. One student who went through our elementary immersion school tells an excellent story about utilizing his language skill and cultural awareness. Mitchell played on the baseball team his freshman year of high school. In one game the opposing team had a new starting pitcher, Javier, who did not speak English. The umpire called this pitcher for a balk. Both the umpire and the coach tried to explain to the young player what he was doing wrong, but could not make him understand. The game continued and the pitcher balked repeatedly. Mitchell's coach then asked if anyone on the team could speak Spanish. Mitchell felt confident in his skills and volunteered. He approached the mound along with the coaches and umpires and began to explain the rules to Javier in Spanish. "It was pretty awesome to just know that I can use (Spanish) on a daily basis, and it was cool to realize I was helping him out," Mitchell said. Javier seemed surprised but also happy that someone could understand and speak with him and gave Mitchell a "thumbs-up" later when he got a hit off of him (Chrapek 2016).

Another student, Auden, reported a different experience playing soccer against a team with all Spanish speakers. The opposing team called out plays to each other in Spanish and couldn't figure out how the non-Latino kid always knew where they were going with the ball. Former students in both Minnesota and Michigan have shared with me many similar stories of using their second language as a "secret" communication tool on athletic fields and ball courts. Likewise, students give numerous accountings of using their language skills to communicate both at home and abroad. The skill is not just a learned academic skill but rather a useful instrument packed away in their knowledge tool belt, waiting to be put into use as opportunity arises, something that occurs more often than one might think.

> *"For me, whatever academic advantages there were, the ability to communicate with others and the potential for that impact made the immersion program invaluable." – Lisa M, Language Immersion Parent*

The experience gained from having both cross-cultural knowledge and language proficiency is life changing. Parents and students see and feel these results. Educators recognize these strengths in their students every day. "It gives them access to a larger palette of colors with which to paint their world." (Jackson, Kolb and Wilson 2011)

> *"I believe my parents thought it would give me an advantage that other students could not have. I think they were right." – Former Language Immersion Student*

Immersion graduates believe strongly in the impact of their educational experience. They do not take it for granted, though many of them state that they didn't realize that their education was so completely different and beneficial until they went away to college and saw evidence of what they had gained compared to their peers.

> *"No other aspect of my education, and I attended one of the top universities in the country, had as significant of an impact on who I am, how I view the world, and how I live my life than learning Spanish starting in kindergarten has. My passion for languages and love of other cultures was cultivated in the classrooms of (language immersion)....These experiences introduced me to people, ideas, and ways of life I otherwise wouldn't have been exposed to, and it's given me a chance to stretch my comfort zones and learn who I am and push myself to be the best that I can be. I have known Spanish for as long as I can remember, and I honestly cannot imagine a version of me who doesn't know Spanish. There is no question that language immersion is with me every day, even nearly 30 years after I first walked into Señora Martinez' classroom because Spanish is a part of my everyday life and career." – Former Language Immersion Student*

This student's viewpoint comes much later, at the end of the formal language immersion education experience. Though there is an entire chapter devoted to the lifetime impact on immersion graduates, it is important to note now, in the decision-making phase of your experience, that language immersion will positively influence the development of your child academically, developmentally, socially, and culturally. It will likewise influence your whole family. I have never come across an immersion graduate who did not feel the positive impact of early language learning and cultural exposure. In fact, the majority of students use the words "thankful," "grateful," "priceless opportunities" or "open doors" when reminiscing about the impact of immersion on their lives. They often mention their parents with gratitude and awe and appreciation for their foresight.

> *"It was the best thing my parents did for me."*

> *"I would not be where I am today without the decision my parents made and the wonderful environment language immersion was for its students."*

> *"I find that I am overwhelmed by the advantages it has afforded me. When people wonder about schools for their kids I always speak passionately about immersion education. It makes me very sad to know my son won't have that kind of opportunity in the districts in our area."*

Give your child this gift. You will be so glad you did.

CHAPTER 3
The First Year Experience

Your child is now enrolled in the language immersion program and is ready to embark on this great adventure. The anticipation of starting the program builds over the summer, inducing great excitement for the whole family. Your child doesn't really understand exactly what is happening, but knows it's a big deal. When my older son was about to enter language immersion kindergarten, I overheard him talking on the phone one day with his beloved Aunt Julie. She was asking him about starting school and how excited he must be. I heard him reply, "Well you know, I'm going to the Spanish *Emergency* School."

What? Even though my career was devoted to language immersion, it had never occurred to me that he didn't know the word "immersion" and what it meant. It's not exactly a word used by a five-year-old to describe anything in his experience. When I later became a school administrator, I shared that story every year at Kindergarten Roundup and encouraged parents to talk a little bit about "immersion" in non-scary terms. "Immersion is like when you are dunked underwater," is not exactly a comforting thought to a five-year-old. Instead, I encourage parents to talk about immersion as meaning "surrounded by" or "all around you" and to use a variety of examples. You could demonstrate with your hand in a bowl of popcorn saying, "My hand is immersed in popcorn.

The popcorn is all around my hand." Another example might be turning up the music on the car radio and proclaiming, "We are immersed in the music. The music is all around us." Whatever method you use, it might be worth a small discussion about the term "immersion." Let your child know they will be "surrounded by language." Even though I encourage this discussion, I failed to learn this lesson myself early on. When my younger child started immersion kindergarten four years later and had the same phone call with his Aunt Julie, he announced, "I'm going to the Spanish *Virgin* School." Ah, the creativeness of young ears! Obviously, these were ears that were going to benefit from a rich elementary language experience.

Other than possibly spending time introducing the word "immersion," which your child will no doubt hear repeatedly, there really is little needed in the way of preparation to enter the immersion school. Teachers' suggestions include simple interactions with your child: starting to listen to Spanish music and videos, using Spanish apps to introduce the concept of another language, playing memory or strategy board games to work on turn-taking and perseverance, and working on listening skills and respectful behavior. Time you spend practicing the appropriate use of glue and scissors is greatly appreciated by kindergarten teachers as well.

Many parents of successfully transitioned students claim that they did very little to prepare their children for immersion kindergarten. It is not that different from heading off to any kindergarten. As far as your child knows, school is always taught in another language. Some of my former students, when on vacation, had the opportunity to visit the school of their cousins. When they returned to our school they came to my office to inform me, "They don't learn anything in other schools! The teachers just speak in English." It is amusing that students don't recognize that their peers who receive instruction in English are also learning academics. They just don't make the connection that "school" doesn't necessarily equate to "learning another language." They don't know that their education is a special experience when they first begin. Remember, they don't have another kindergarten background to compare with their immersion education.

> *"I didn't prepare to be honest. I didn't tell him anything. I didn't make a big deal about it. He just went. As my oldest, he didn't know any different until a couple of weeks later when he noticed the kids in the other kindergarten weren't speaking Spanish." – Catherine C-H, Language Immersion Parent*

> *"We did nothing special except get him ready for being away from home during the day." – Language Immersion Parent*

> *"For both of our children the idea was that school was that way and that they were very lucky to be included in this exciting program." – Language Immersion Parent*

> *"We did tell him that he would be learning in Spanish but really, preparation was the same as we would have done for English kindergarten. Our next two children were just going to go there: no question." – Jan L, Language Immersion Parent*

> *"I didn't prepare him. I threw him to the wolves and he did great!" – Krista F, Language Immersion Parent*

The first day is the biggest step you will face. This is true for any kindergarten parent, but somehow you know that this first drop-off at immersion school or at the bus stop is really a big thing. This one act will change your child forever. A former immersion student who is now also an immersion teacher shared,

"I tell parents that my mom recently confessed to me, 'When we put you on that bus the first day, we knew that the entire trajectory of your life could change.' My mom's prediction was so true. Most of the big decisions and experiences I have had in my life have been directly connected to what I have learned through immersion education. I tell new immersion parents that they are doing a brave thing and that if they take the brave first step and continue to support their child through it, immersion education will make all the difference in the life of their child." – Allison M, Language Immersion Educator and Former Student

Acquiring Language in the First Year

The first year is undoubtedly the most amazing year in immersion education for parents. You know in your head what is supposed to happen. You've read the goals, done your research, attended the parent meetings, listened to the principal and teachers explain procedures, yet everything surprises you in the early days. You will pick up your child at school or visit for a special event and witness your child listening to an adult speaking rapidly in the target language. Then you will see your child respond either verbally or by completing an action to follow directions, and you will be amazed. Again, you know this is supposed to happen in your brain, but you're not quite prepared for that leap in your heart when you see your child begin to thrive in the target language. This is particularly true if you do not speak a second language yourself or if you studied a language with limited success. You are elated that this is so natural a process for your child! I have observed this early acquisition of language for more than three decades. It still thrills me every single time I witness fresh kindergarteners start to respond to directions in a new language.

Let's remember that children develop competence in their first language before coming to school. They already have strategies for interaction, asking and giving information, participating in conversation, and expressing wants and needs (Saville-Troike, McClure and Fritz 1984). In school, students first respond using English. They soon start using their new language to implement those very strategies they developed before reaching school age. It's so easy for them!

> In normal language development, children have between 2,500 and 5,000 words by age six. Thus, the reason why students do not flinch when they are amidst the ambiguity of the language immersion classroom is because they are used to continuously encountering new words in their native language. When learning his/her own language, children rarely ask what a word means. It is the same in the immersion classroom. They are literally accustomed to uncertainty and novelty. (Carver-Akers 2013)

The first part of the year you may be thinking, "I'm going to learn French along with my child. I can do this too." You will find that you will be able to learn the language with your child as they begin the program. However, I must issue a fair warning: soon it will become apparent that your child is indeed a sponge and is soaking the language up at a far greater rate than you are. You start falling behind bit by bit. Then, it's a runaway train and you are left standing at the station. As adults, we simply don't acquire language as quickly as children do. We also do not have the hours of exposure each day that they do. If you invested 6-7 hours, five days a week, nine months a year—you too would gain competence. Still, you would have to work harder than your child to acquire only a percentage of the skills your child will master.

This is not to say that you should not try to also learn the language. Acquiring language skills benefits everyone, no matter their age, so learn what you can. It has even been proposed that late language learning may help delay dementia. While this may not be on your horizon yet, good health probably is, so go for it. Don't be afraid to try to read with your child any materials that come home. Yes, you will mispronounce things or use a strange accent, but this leads to a wonderful transformation. Your child becomes the teacher. Your son may laugh at your strange speaking of "his" language and most assuredly will correct you. Go with that flow.

> "I once told my mom, 'You're saying the right words, but your words sound crooked.'" – Auden R, Language Immersion Student

Correction of your language is justified and helps reinforce the learning at school. Let your child see you work at the language alongside them. Allow your child to be the "expert" in your house. Show support for the learning that is happening and this will serve as nourishment for the seeds planted at school.

In the first part of kindergarten, teachers emphasize oral skills. Teachers speak the target language exclusively and your child listens, understands and responds. This is what is known in the language-learning profession as "comprehensible input," (Krashen 1984), language that is needed for acquisition. The teacher will be giving instructions and holding conversations in the target language and your child will listen, comprehend and then respond to the teacher in English.

> It would be unnatural and frustrating for early immersion education students to be prevented from using their first language in the initial months of schooling. The use of English is therefore permitted among the students.... The focus is on conveying content and responding to the substance of what the students are saying, regardless of the fact that students' early communication is in their home

> language, English. This approach results in meaningful verbal interaction based on the realities of the child's life and the relatively concrete, context-embedded activities that occur in a kindergarten or first grade classroom. (Lapkin and Cummins 1984)

Students may continue to use English with each other both in learning and play settings, but little by little the target language will start to creep in, and they will begin to use their second language without being aware they are doing so.

Student use of the target language varies, so there is no reason to be concerned if your child starts responding later. In fact, researchers at the University of Illinois found that some of the students who sat and watched rather than engaging in speaking early on actually did better in the long run. The children who began to speak in the target language later often did so with complex sentences (Saville-Troike, McClure and Fritz 1984). This is interesting data and confirms what practitioners know: that children vary greatly and they all learn in their own way and their own time. Don't worry if your child isn't using the new language as soon as another child. Information is being processed and cataloged differently than it is by the child who expresses that information out loud.

> Speaking is a *result* of acquisition; the ability to speak a second language "emerges" or develops on its own only after the acquirer has built up enough competence by listening and reading. This hypothesis explains why children often go through a silent period of several months before they begin to speak a new language. This silent period is a time during which they are building competence in the second language—when they begin to speak, it is not the beginning of their acquisition, just the beginning of showing off their competence. (Krashen 1984)

It actually may be a while before you start hearing target language production at home. This is completely normal. Children generally are not required to use the target language independently until the second half of first grade. At that time they will be encouraged gently to use it more and more to express themselves. When a student responds in English, the teacher may feign a lack of understanding, and the child will usually make an instantaneous switch to the target language. In kindergarten however, students are still in that silent acquisition phase where they listen, listen, listen and start comprehending very quickly.

> *"Be patient. There is often a 'silent period' before kids start speaking in their new language. It will happen, and it will be great!"*
> – Mary Jeanne S, Language Immersion Teacher and Parent

The Kindergarten Curriculum

There are planned activities in kindergarten when children are encouraged to spend time orally practicing their new language. Most classes begin the day with a morning meeting or a "carpet time" where many concepts of the kindergarten curriculum are taught. Students initially repeat, and later list independently, vocabulary words related to calendar, weather, numbers, birthdays, and any other number of vocabulary sets. Often they learn to sing and chant, activities in which they are learning early phonics skills that will help them when they begin to read. Learning topics are introduced through direct instruction with the whole class, as well as guided interaction between students in the target language.

Just as in traditional kindergarten classrooms, whole class time is often followed by small group instruction, where students interact further, or open class time for exploration of learning centers. Often there is differentiated instruction, in which some students receive more guidance and practice, while others can work on challenging activities after mastering the current topic being explored (Zachmeier-Ruh and Bausman-Watkins 2005). Immersion teachers give students a lot of encouragement and positively reinforce any target language production from them. As a rule, teachers do not correct errors the children make in the language, but model the language correctly when responding to the student. In this manner, the child is encouraged to continue to take risks using the language and also hears the language used repeatedly in the correct form by the teacher. An example in English would be if your child said to you, "Me want the blue one." As a parent you might say, "You want the blue one? Well, *I* want the yellow one." You don't stop to correct your child; you just answer using correct structure. You do this naturally. Immersion teachers follow this same pattern in the target language, continually modeling the correct use of the target language. Many immersion students are extremely surprised the first time they overhear their teacher speaking English, such as with parents, because they didn't realize the teacher spoke English. It makes me smile to recall the looks of amazement on students' faces at this discovery. Yes, their mouths literally hang open as they switch gazes from parent to teacher and back again.

Again, if you don't hear your child speak the target language very much the first year, don't panic. This is normal language acquisition. Your child is doing what they should be doing—learning and cataloging an enormous vocabulary that will pop out naturally when they are ready. And then watch out! It will be very exciting. Do you remember when this child was a very young toddler and did not speak very much, but understood a lot of what you said to them? Before you knew it, they were speaking in full sentences, all the time. Your child goes through this same listening stage in kindergarten and progresses with learning speech in the second language in a natural manner.

The process of speaking varies so much with children, depending on factors such as personality, risk-taking, developmental levels, and actual age (there is sometimes a full year or more difference in the ages of kindergarten children). Children who speak early in English often also speak early in the target language; likewise for those who speak later in both languages. But then again, children are known to surprise us and sooner or later will use the language more frequently both inside and outside the classroom. For example, of third and fourth grade Spanish immersion students surveyed, 84% indicated that they speak the target language outside school (Pool 2003). This process starts in kindergarten with listening, then speaking, and increases over time until students are comfortable speaking both their languages in any appropriate setting. Hang in there, because you are bound to overhear your child speak their new language at some point.

Another important part of the kindergarten curriculum is the development of pre-reading skills. Your child will learn the alphabet and sound system of the target language. Phonics development is an important part of many of the languages being learned as well. Emphasis will be placed on reading skills such as scanning left to right and top to bottom (in many languages—or right to left for some languages), associating text with sounds, possibly recognizing word shapes, and many other pre-reading skills. The specific type of pre-reading skill development is normally a district-wide decision and the immersion program will typically follow the educational approach being utilized at other schools in your district. Whether phonics, whole language, or any other combination of approaches or techniques, this is big stuff!

Reading is the key, the base upon which all learning throughout the educational experience will occur. Kindergarten and first grade is the time when this miracle begins to appear, and it will happen for your child in a second language. You will see library books and other reading materials come home with your child, and you can spend many lovely hours perusing them together. This is an opportunity to witness beginning performance in the target language as your child's skills increase bit by bit.

Your child may also start early writing during the kindergarten year. In the beginning this will be mostly copying of text, in which your child will simply rewrite letters, symbols, words and text provided by the teacher. Pattern sentences with creative word substitutions will follow. For example, a student may write, "I like" and then choose from a list of vocabulary words for an ending to the sentence. Writing skill builds through the year. By the month of May, your child may be able to create a classic Mother's Day card written in the target language, through a guided writing activity.

In addition to the important skills of reading and writing, your child will also be learning content in math, science, and social studies, all taught in the target language. For example in addition to learning numbers, counting by 2's, 5's and 10's, your child will learn beginning concepts in geometry shapes, measurement, and basic operations in math. In science, topics might include animals, plants, weather and (yes!) data collection. Social Studies may offer discussions of timelines, graphs, maps, flags, directions, and citizenship to name a few. There will be a significant amount of vocabulary learning in these lessons, and your child will also be learning important skills and gaining new information that is all part of the regular kindergarten curriculum.

Parents and Language Learning

Research for 50 years has documented the impact of parent attitudes on children's success at learning language, particularly at the elementary level (Feenstra 1969; Gardner 1968; Colletta, Clement and Edwards 1983). Do not doubt for a minute that your child picks up your attitudes about language learning. If you love learning languages or simply are fascinated by the idea of language learning, your child will reflect this love and natural curiosity. If, on the other hand, you have bad memories of your own language learning, you will easily convey these feelings to your child as well. Be careful to be positive, enthusiastic, and most of all, brave! Your child will internalize these feelings and transfer them to their own experience, making the first year more fun and enjoyable for the entire family.

> *"I would suggest that parents understand and are prepared for the long-term commitment immersion education requires. There will be times when their child will love immersion and times when they do not... The best way to make the transition for kids easier is to always be positive about the experience, focus on the positive gifts, provide many opportunities to support use of their language outside the classroom and frequently celebrate language learning." – Patrick S, Language Immersion Teacher*

There are also parents who already speak the language their child is learning, or at least have studied it before. Your child may come home having learned a different word or expression than you use in your vocabulary. That's ok! How "brown" is said in one country or region may be different from the term in another. If, for example, your child is learning Spanish, your child may say *café*, *marrón*, or *pardo* or use any number of other terms. Variety and language diversity is part of the learning process. Don't correct your child but let them know that you use a different word, and that it's ok to use both. The past experiences of your child's teachers, teaching assistants and other staff working at the school, including studying and living in a particular country or growing up in a native-speaking family, will all influence the vocabulary your child learns and uses. How wonderful that your child will be exposed to a variety of language dialects and backgrounds!

My older son spent a summer in Spain with me after his second grade year in language immersion. We were having dinner with a family in Sevilla and John was seated at the opposite end of the table from the family patriarch. The father asked my son a question but John was seated so far away he couldn't hear well. He stood up and leaned over the table and said "*¿Mande?*" upon which the entire table broke out in laughter. They understood that John was saying "What?" but he was using a term that his second grade teacher who had lived in Mexico used rather than "*¿Cómo?*" as a Spaniard might say. Despite the good-natured laughter, the family assured John that they were very impressed that his command of the language included a variety of terms to express a thought. John had no feelings of self-consciousness or embarrassment about saying something differently. Instead, he felt very proud of knowing something unique and was encouraged to use his language further with native speakers. This was one of those amazing parent moments when we get to witness our children demonstrating competence and accomplishment. This particular experience happened naturally, in an authentic setting, when John was still a young language learner.

Over my career, I have had many parents share stories with me of their children interpreting not only when traveling abroad but also in local situations. One immersion family had friends who were providing Christmas dinner for a family in need. The friends found that the family only spoke Spanish so they asked the second grade immersion student for help. The student was able to communicate and made all of the arrangements with the Spanish-speaking family for delivery of the dinner (Hillary 2007). One parent shared the story of her child who was called in from the waiting room to translate for her dentist who was trying to communicate a procedure with a Spanish-speaking patient. Another student shared a story of being in line at a grocery store with her parents. The woman ahead of them in line was not speaking Spanish, the language of the child's immersion program, but was clearly having trouble communicating with the cashier while speaking her native language. The child, having learned to listen, take risks, and guess with language, stepped up and proclaimed to the cashier, "What she is trying to tell you is…." and then proceeded to help resolve the communication problem. The parents watched in amazement at the confidence their child showed in understanding communication in a foreign language she didn't know, a skill attributed to the immersion experience. The child viewed this as a completely natural interaction. It was a true communicative experience even though the immersion *language* was not used, but immersion *skills* were employed.

As parents, especially in the first year, we want to hear the results of our child's learning. Quite frankly, we want to hear them speak a foreign language fluently. Sometimes other relatives want to hear this skill as well. They want proof that this alternative way of learning is actually accomplishing something, forgetting that the child is learning the entire regular kindergarten curriculum as well. The result is constant pressure being placed on the child to say something in the target language or respond to questions such as, "What is this in French?" These are demands that are quite unnatural to the child. They simply do not see you as a native speaker, and therefore do not see how it serves a purpose to speak the language with you.

> *"My kids would tell people that they don't translate in the way that non-speakers assume. They simply knew what things were or how to say that almost subconsciously. They weren't ready to respond to calls to make that conscious until they were older." – Lisa M, Language Immersion Parent*

So, especially at first, be patient and wait. Soon enough there will be school programs and other opportunities for you to visit your child in the school setting, and you will be amazed by what you see and hear. Don't force your child to "perform" for you or other friends and family. Don't push the "Say something in French for Aunt Josephine" agenda. Unless Aunt Josephine also speaks French, this is not a normal language setting for the child. Let your children initiate their own conversations with target language-speaking friends and family. Of course, behind the scenes feel free to let French-speaking Aunt Josephine know that she can initiate a target language discussion with your child, but warn her not to force any interaction that doesn't flow naturally.

Another example of unduly pushing your budding language learner might be to insist that your child order for the table in Spanish at a Mexican restaurant. Really? Would your child order for the table in any other restaurant? Again, this is not a natural language setting for your child and will lead to frustration on everyone's part. On the other hand, if your child shows interest in speaking the target language with waiters, cooks, or any native speaker, feel free to encourage and support this behavior. Also, if you happen to be traveling to a target language country, community, or other similar setting, and don't have the language skills you need, feel free to ask your child for assistance. Your child will sense that this is an authentic setting that validates the usage of their language skills.

One immersion student was traveling during spring break with his family. He wore his school T-shirt with Spanish text on it. His grandparents, who had previously expressed interest in his immersion experience, were traveling with them. In the past, he had refused to perform on command so his grandparents could hear him speak Spanish. On this trip, en route to dinner and escorted only by his grandparents, a Dominican called out in Spanish, "Hey gringo, that's a cool shirt—where did you get it?" Without hesitation, the six year old fired back in Spanish, "At my school in Michigan we only speak Spanish. This is my school t-shirt." Both the Dominican and the grandparents were both surprised and impressed.

This story provides a great example of immersion students selecting when and where they feel speaking the target language is appropriate. The student had the language skills all along—he just waited for a situation that he felt legitimately required a response in Spanish. Likewise, let your child lead in using their language skills outside of school in a way that feels comfortable and natural for them. Allow your child to enjoy being a delightful five or six-year-old who enjoys the immersion experience and basks in learning this new language without undue pressure. If they wish to use the target language, enjoy! If they prefer to keep it to themselves and not perform for your ears, or to impress your family and friends, be patient. The day may come when you wish your child *would* speak in English!

Because my husband and I also spoke Spanish, my children could never resort to using the target language as a "secret tool" in front of us. Other parents have reported that the day comes when their children speak Spanish together as a way of communicating in a private manner around their parents.

> *"Our neighbor told us that her daughters would speak to each other in Spanish when they wanted to hide something from their parents." – Lisa M, Language Immersion Parent*

> *"I had a fair amount of Spanish experience, and though not fluent, I could comprehend much of what my students were saying. The third graders were in the process of explaining to me how "boletos" (tickets) worked when they were rewarded for using a lot of Spanish in their classroom. They thought I should use them as well and that would help my Spanish also. These eight year olds were arguing completely in Spanish! I was astounded! I thought 'Wow! This is incredible! My own kids will be able to argue with one another in English AND Spanish!' and then I gave it another thought, 'This is a good thing???? Ah, yes. Yes, it is!'" – Kathleen P, Language Immersion Music Educator and Parent*

"Our son said to his girlfriend, 'Our children will be able to speak Spanish.' And then he laughed and said, 'Then we can talk and you won't know what we are saying. Just like when my sisters and I talked in Spanish when we didn't want my Mom knowing what we were talking about!'" – Sandra B-S, Language Immersion Parent

If you really want to hear more developing language skills in the early days, ask your child's teacher if there is a way you can volunteer to help in the classroom. There you will have the opportunity to hear the entire class in action (more on this in Chapter 7). Quite possibly you will get lucky, like the parent who went upstairs to check on her daughter, who was in bed. The sleeping girl sat up and started speaking in Spanish to her mother, who only spoke English. The mother claimed, "That's serious immersion!"

Social Development

This first year you may see your child blossom with self-confidence. Children enter immersion programs with varying levels of social skills and this can influence their willingness to experiment with the language. Students mostly enter kindergarten as monolinguals, so they are on equal footing with respect to the target language, though maybe not equal in their level of confidence. It doesn't matter if Jason could read before kindergarten and Tony was showing no interest in the printed word. When they walk through those school doors for the first time, most children are at the same point in learning the new language. These new kindergarten students show tremendous growth in confidence and become proud of their language experience very quickly. It's fun to outshine mom and dad in at least this one area. Your child may become more knowledgeable than you in this domain. Are you ok with your child having more expertise in something—their new language—than you? Parents need self-confidence too.

This is not to say that you will never see frustration or tears. If your child comes home in tears, it is probably based on a problem other than the language. Children who cry in language immersion kindergarten most likely would cry in an English-only kindergarten as well. I often tell parents the first thing to look for is tiredness. Kindergarten is tiring for all children. It's a new experience and it quite frankly wears them out. Then, there is the language input for seven hours a day. Your child is paying special attention and it is exhausting. This tiredness will be prevalent in kindergarten and often continues into first grade, when children are learning to read.

As one student told his first grade teacher, "*Voy a casa a dormir mucho. No me siento bien y mi cabeza va a explotar.*" (I'm going home to sleep a lot. I don't feel well and my head is going to explode.) Yes, it can wear out kids enough to make them feel not only tired, but sick as well. It's normal. If you have ever lived in another country where you don't speak the language well, you know what I'm talking about. It's exhausting to stay alert constantly, listening for communication. Try to find downtime for a nap if possible. By all means, get your child to bed early. Parents have at times been horrified when I suggested an 8 p.m. bedtime, but then come back later to thank me when they discover that this solved the problem.

"The kids will be exhausted. Spending the whole day in a second language is VERY tiring for a while. It takes time to adjust to the immersion environment, just as any adjustment takes time. Make sure the kids get lots of rest and lots of love and encouragement at home. Don't push them too much." – Laura M, Language Immersion Teacher

"Be patient! Language learning is hard work and children get tired, but their minds are capable and it is worth it!" – Kally C, Language Immersion Teacher

> *"Kids need extra sleep, reassurance and support when hitting the wall in kindergarten. Keep a positive attitude and it will help them to think positively as well."* – Rebecca G, Language Immersion Teacher

The first year is a joy. Though you may have initial fears and concerns, you will be at an amazing place by the end of the year. You will have a child in your home that can understand native speakers in a new language with ease. Your child will have already developed an acceptance and interest in people different from your family. Your child will also have mastered the first year of regular school curriculum and be well prepared to continue immersion education successfully throughout elementary school.

> *"I loved the sense of community – similar to what you get at a private school. Learning content in a second language enhanced my learning comprehension, academic skill set, and provided knowledge and passion for learning about diverse cultures and travel."*
> – Micki C, Language Immersion Student

The gift you have chosen to give your child and your family will have already started to blossom by the time the first year is over, with only more joys and successes to follow. You will already know that you definitely made the right choice in an educational program.

CHAPTER 4
Growing Through the Elementary Grades

My brother and I are very different but we both benefitted from immersion education. I think my parents could see the benefits even from the beginning so any extra sacrifice (of which the only one I can think of was the extra long bus ride) was worth it." – Ellen T, Former Language Immersion Student

You made it through the beginning year! You have exploded with joy over your child's increasing skills in a new language. Your visits to the school have reassured you that your child is receiving an amazing educational experience. Now it's time to grow into that most important academic period of elementary school: grades 1-5.

There are two very important things to keep in mind about this time. One, your child is first and foremost a child. This is the single most important aspect of these years. Your child has only one opportunity to enjoy the ages of 5-10. Avoid too much pressure, and throw yourself into enjoying the physical, emotional, and cognitive growth that occurs during these years. Secondly, these years form the academic base for everything that follows in life and therefore are really, really important.

Sounds like these contradict each other, right? Yes, it seems that way. Both statements are valid, and while they appear opposing, they really are a call for balance during these years. Support the academic growth and make sure it becomes firmly rooted. At the same time, ensure that your child has time to be a young individual who is naturally interested in the surrounding world, and seeks play and exploration.

Elizabeth Weise, in her *A Parent's Guide to Mandarin Immersion* (2014) describes what she calls "The First Grade Freak-Out." As a former elementary principal, I had to laugh at her terminology, largely because I know exactly what she is talking about. This is truly the phenomenon that occurs once the family has grown accustomed to, and is possibly "over," their child's amazing initial success in the language developed in kindergarten. Parents are still delighted daily with their child's increasing language skill, but now academics in the content areas start to become more pressing to parents, and the focus shifts a bit. Many parents can't resist comparing their child with English-only peers, which leads to the freak-out. The principal area of concern is progress made in English.

> *"Teachers want parents to just trust them, but parents want a little assurance that their child is going to be all right in this second language environment. Both are understandable. A balance is necessary which can be achieved through open, consistent and empathetic communication." – Laura M, Language Immersion Teacher*

> *"One of the biggest struggles was learning not to compare my daughter to her peers who were at traditional schools." – Michelle C, Language Immersion Parent*

> *"Our family did well. The hardest thing for us personally was not giving in to the 'passionate parent' mentality and just trusting the system." – Kristin B, Language Immersion Parent*

English

I always have presented parents with reams of research about the results of language immersion studies. Parents go home from Kindergarten Roundup or visits to the school office armed with articles about the success of immersion programs in general, and our own program in particular. These results are most likely available from the school you are checking into, and the Internet is filled with information documenting general immersion success. At the end of this book, you will find a list of resources that offer all the information you could want to ease your mind about immersion success, including results on the English development of elementary immersion students.

In a survey of parents at the Ada Vista Spanish Immersion program, 73% said that their children made the transition from Spanish reading to English reading on their own. Most parents indicated however that they "coached" their children by reading to their children every night, pointing out signs while driving, and using reading readiness computer games. One parent in the survey noted that she read 20 minutes of English and 20 minutes of Spanish each night. Others stated that their children appeared to learn English reading right along with their Spanish reading (Hillary 2007).

Indeed, I have observed numerous children who appear to "magically" learn to read in English overnight when this subject is formally introduced in the second grade. Although it appears to be magical, these children have been learning to read in English all along. The reading skills they have gained in the target language transfer to their native language. In addition, for the past six years they have been amazingly observant of text around them in the world. On their own, they apply their target language reading skills to English, which explains a few interesting pronunciations of words when they first begin reading, providing smiles and laughter to themselves and others.

> *"Emily and I were riding in our van when she was in kindergarten. She began reading signs along the road, translating them from English to Spanish, as we were driving. That was pretty cool, but then I nearly fell off my seat when she looked down at what she was holding and pronounced it in Spanish - Bar-Bee-eh. Barbie. Too funny!"* – Kathleen P, Language Immersion Parent and Educator

> *"We understood that English would come along with the Spanish. That was our experience with all three children. When the key to reading was unlocked in Spanish, it was also unlocked for them in English. We read to them in both languages before bed. The only issue that we had occasionally was the mispronunciation of an English word. This still happens."* – Jan L, Language Immersion Parent

> *"I had no fears about English, but was surprised when she sounded out English words with Spanish language pronunciation."* – Language Immersion Parent

Whether or not one supports all the testing that typically occurs in schools, parents generally want their children to perform well when those assessments are given. In addition, school districts generally want to know that students in all their school buildings are meeting standards and outcomes. Results for nearly 40 years have consistently found that language immersion students gain English skills on a par with students in English-only programs, and most often have test scores that surpass their monolingual peers. Mandated state testing, additional achievement tests, and local district testing all bear similar results, giving immersion education solid support in preparing students for the rigors of high-stakes testing programs. In addition, taking writing assessments in English, one of the most difficult skills to master for *all* students, is no more difficult for immersion students. In very early immersion programs beginning in the 70s it was reported that fourth grade immersion students lagged behind English program students in spelling, but the stories of the immersion students were more original and rated more highly in sentence accuracy, vocabulary choice, sentence complexity and variety, and overall organization (Genesee quoted in Swain 1984). The skills noted by Genesee as ranking higher are those that bear the greater importance when students write college essay applications and pursue collegiate study. Spelling can be corrected as students gain self-editing skills throughout the educational sequence.

> *"I wasn't worried about my kids' English. I know the research. Reading and writing are transferable skills." – Jennifer H, Language Immersion Parent*

> *"I was a little afraid they'd be behind in English but that was proven wrong by second grade." – Beth D, Language Immersion Parent*

> *"I worried I would be behind in English but did not find that to be the case. Plenty of exposure to English outside of school." – Micki C, Former Language Immersion Student*

> *"They catch up and surpass. Life outside school is English immersion. Read in English at home and all is good." – Language Immersion Parent*

Concern often increases when children attend classes and programs outside of school and find themselves in classrooms with students from English-only programs. Parents start to see their child compared with others, usually in first or second grade, and sometimes an unaware instructor makes a comment about poor spelling. These horrified and embarrassed parents come running back to the school, doubting their immersion choice. They often request remediation for their child or changes in the curriculum to "correct" this problem. Then, third grade happens! Most children start to catch up to their peers in spelling in third grade, and by fourth grade may even start to pull ahead. And don't forget, these same children also spell very well in a second language, something their English-only peers cannot do.

"Early on this was the hardest area for me. The kids all seemed to pick up English at different speeds. In particular it was hard not to compare to other kids who were in traditional schools. They were reading in English before her, reading chapter books before her. I felt fearful whether she would catch up. Now that it's been several years I can see that I just needed to be patient and confident in the model." – Michelle C, Language Immersion Parent

"No issues with English at all. I've been an avid reader and even got to the state spelling bee in middle school." – Anita M, Former Language Immersion Student

"I wasn't worried about English but my extended family was. Her spelling lagged behind but now she is in junior high and she seems right at average along with being able to write in Spanish too." – Language Immersion Parent

Parents do need to exercise patience and realize that though they may see a delay in this one skill area, it will not last. In fact, children were tested in spelling at both the beginning and end of first grade in a French immersion school. Results showed that spelling errors were more basic at the beginning of the year and more complex at the end of the year in both languages. In spite of being taught in French, with no direct instruction in English, spelling skills developed in the native language, suggesting that these skills transfer between languages (Joy 2011). Again, this study was completed with first grade students, quite early in the process, and before English instruction even starts in an immersion program. Imagine how much more quickly students learn English spelling skills once direct instruction occurs. English spelling skills are merely delayed, not impaired.

The delay occurs because your child is focusing on developing other skills at this time. That spelling demon is conquered soon enough. It is interesting to note, however, that many language immersion graduates, when recalling their learning of English, do remember struggling, principally with grammar and spelling. They did not become aware of these issues, however, until they were in secondary school and entered classrooms with students from English-only programs. Nearly all students indicate that they quickly caught up with their peers and that it worked out well for them. Other students do not recall any issues with learning English.

> *"I do not feel my English suffered at all. We had enough time devoted to learning English that I never felt behind any of my peers who did not attend immersion." – Ellen T, Former Language Immersion Student*

> *"In early English classes I struggled but I quickly made up for it." – Former Language Immersion Student*

> *"I never had any fears about learning English (reading, writing, academic language) well. I feel that my English abilities developed alongside my Spanish abilities with few to no difficulties." – Allison M, Former Language Immersion Student and Teacher*

> *"The funniest was when our daughter was in first grade reading a stop sign with a Spanish accent, ESTOP. We weren't fearful. We knew that would come. Our daughter scored VERY high on the ACT for the essay portion and her writing and grammar are*

superb. As grammar lovers ourselves, my husband and I are excited that this love of language and language syntax, connections, etc. lives on in both our kids." – Marla B, Language Immersion Parent

Parents should also note that many, many students have commented that their knowledge of the second language gives them a base that they are able to apply to spelling and other English skills later on. Students' knowledge of English improves due to having a comparative platform that helps them analyze language. This happens particularly in high school when they are working more with the "rules" of the English language. Students do not say that the second language hindered their ability in English, but rather feel it enhanced their understanding of how language works. A study by Lindholm-Leary (2016a) conducted in dual-language immersion programs, including both Spanish and Mandarin programs, gathered information regarding students' perspectives on their experience. These students expressed that being bilingual helps them think more creatively and that learning a second language has helped them understand their first language better.

"I feel it helped me to understand difficult vocabulary and terminology both in English and French, as the Latin roots of words were familiar to me from Spanish." – Allison M, Language Immersion Educator and Former Student

"I felt more prepared once I entered high school and saw how it directly affected my writing and understanding in English classes." – Morgan P, Former Language Immersion Student

"I do not feel that I was hindered by attending an immersion program. In fact, in high school I was in honors English and AP English for all four years and excelled in those courses. – John M, Former Language Immersion Student

"It has made me love languages and the history of where words came from. I love being able to switch back and forth so easily between languages. It has given me an even greater variety of words to express myself in English and Spanish." – Former Language Immersion Student

In the early sixties I did not have the benefit of a language immersion experience. However, I was fortunate to have a second grade teacher, the inspirational Mrs. Bachelder, who taught Spanish vocabulary to our class for a few minutes every day. I diligently kept a notebook as my Spanish dictionary and lapped up those new words with great thirst. I was a very good speller, winning my school spelling bee each year. I remember with great clarity that the word I spelled to win the third grade championship was "chocolate." Many who know me now just smile and say, "of course." However, while the runner-up spelled the word "choclate," it was my introduction to Spanish by Mrs. Bachelder that taught me "*cho-co-la-te*" and helped me win the spelling bee. Consider how much more a student in an immersion program can benefit from learning to spell in a second language, linking it to their knowledge of English, and using it as one more resource in their educational storehouse.

Math

Concerns about the development of math skills are generally minimal in the early grades. This is partly due to the fact that math is in itself another language, one parents already know and understand. Parents may not recognize the new language terminology but do understand addition and subtraction, shapes, graphs and other basic concepts. When math homework comes home with target language instructions on the page, parents tend to look at the math work itself and make a leap of understanding. For example, 2 + 2 is the same whether you call it "two plus two" or "*dos más dos.*" Parents tend to experience little or no stress over assisting with math work at home. If a teacher notes a concern with adding, subtracting or another early math skill, parents can jump in and easily provide support through extra practice, math games, or computer programs.

Comfort with math remains the normal experience of kindergarten through third grade parents. Then, all of a sudden, fourth grade math becomes far more language-based and parental fourth grade math mania sets in. Parents start calling each other asking, "Do you get this?" and "What's going on here?" Before long the principal's office is bombarded with parents who are frantic with huge math concerns.

Part of this reaction reflects more than just language discomfort. Parental math anxieties exist in English-only programs as well beginning in fourth grade. Math, as it is taught in schools now, is much less rote practice and memorization and more focused on thinking skills, using new strategies, estimation and, yes, lots of language. Merging math and language skills carries much greater weight today than when most parents attended elementary school. This is due to the now-common task of requiring students to give explanations about math strategies; they must describe the steps and processes they used to arrive at a particular conclusion. This requires a fairly high-level language skill in either language, leading parents to look at that fourth grade math book and exclaim, "What?" They immediately attribute it to the target language. Some parents then beg for an English copy of the math book or go online and purchase one for themselves.

Unfortunately, after investing in that English math book, parents soon find out that it's not just a language concern. It's also a new math strategy issue, and with time their child might begin to understand it on their own. In fact, students often figure it out well before their parents—more of that brain flexibility at work. I do not mean to minimize math concerns. Parents just need to be prepared and expect that math will continue to get more difficult as it increases in language intensity. Again, this happens in English-only schools as well. Actually, learning a new way to do math isn't so bad for anyone, at any age.

The best approach is to stick with it and help your children by being supportive and, above all, calm. That's not to say that calling other parents and asking, "Hey, do you understand chapter 6?" isn't a good idea. Parents who work together to help their children achieve success in school form a strong team. These stressful situations offer a great excuse to have dinner together with other immersion families. You can play after-dinner math games and engage in a great social networking experience.

As students grow older, they sometimes discover they do not know the English words for some of the math terminology. This becomes a concern for them.

"I had a hard time changing math from Spanish to English but after learning the English terms for the Spanish ones I already knew, I became very successful in math." – Former Language Immersion Student

"In my first English math class I realized I didn't have the English vocabulary I needed. It was rectified quickly by asking my immersion homeroom teacher for help, which she gladly provided." – Talley S, Former Language Immersion Student

This gap actually starts to appear in third grade when students are required to complete state assessments in English. The instructions ask them to answer questions, using processes they know perfectly well, but using English terminology, which is unfamiliar to them. As parents, you can help. When you are assisting with math homework, you could say something like, "Oh, this assignment is about 'sets.' I understand now!" Your child will start to pick up these English terms and this will help the transition to English math class later in their education. Don't worry about confusing your child by introducing the English terminology at home. They will file the words separately in their brains and pull them out later as needed. Again, their language processing skills are amazing! Just be casual about it. Don't force them to master the words, but rather provide an English "immersion" experience at home and use the words naturally in your conversation.

Science and Social Studies

These subject areas are just downright fun in any elementary school, and this is true for language immersion programs as well. Often in immersion schools, these subjects have the added interest of focusing on global concerns or on the culture of the target language, while still meeting district and state educational curriculum standards. Because of the rich vocabulary of these content areas, and students' natural curiosity about science and social studies, these subjects offer the best opportunities for expanding students' target language beyond anything they would experience in a language pullout class. Science and social studies topics not only are a wealth of information, they also form vast containers where a great amount of student language development occurs.

From a parent perspective, it is a joy to watch your child come home filled with excitement about the topics being taught in science and social studies. Be prepared to visit museums, find movies, go to the library for more information, and generally expand learning on any topic your child is excited about. Though these activities usually will be in English rather than the target language, the information reinforces that learned in school and adds to your child's interest in the topic on a deeper level. This provides extra fun for the whole family as you engage in continued study about what your child is learning at school.

On the other hand, these two subjects may be the very ones that will require the most assistance from you at home. Often, these are the "project" subjects, where your child will need to work on a larger research project or science experiment, create a book, or prepare a display. Yes, you will need to assist, but you will not be expected to help with the language part of it. Your role is to furnish any and all supplies, help with locating materials, and provide opportunities for the research part of the project. Be present to support, provide snacks, and give lots of encouragement.

Keep in contact with the teacher if you have questions when there are large projects looming. Make sure you have received all the information your child was given on what is required. Most teachers are very explicit with instructions for at-home projects and often give out rubrics or checklists that describe exactly how the project will be graded. Your child will most likely receive this information in the target language but sometimes a copy will come home for you in English or will be posted on the teacher's webpage. You need to tap that communication network you have already established with the teacher to clarify any concerns.

There may be an event at the school, such as a science or history fair, where projects are displayed or students give presentations. Sometimes projects are displayed during parent-teacher conferences or other school events. Take time to attend these events, peruse all the projects, and listen to the presentations. This will give you a good idea of how others approach these assignments. You will gain a better view of teacher expectations and gather ideas for future projects that your child will certainly be required to produce.

Enjoy what your child learns in science and social studies. Your interest will encourage your child. Tap into the excitement and wonder your child expresses and run with it. This is the fun part, the magic, of education. Enjoy!

Music, Physical Education, Art, Health, and More

Often known as "specials," these subjects are sometimes taught in the target language, but often are not, due to available staffing. Many immersion schools have made huge efforts to hunt for staff that can teach these subjects in the target language, but most often this can only occur as job openings become available in the district. It is rare that a district will let current staff go in order to replace with a target language speaker in these subjects. Those schools that can offer these subjects in the target language offer two advantages: one, a greater percentage of the school day is in the target language; and two, the opportunities for developing a wider vocabulary increase with every additional subject offered.

Many times teachers of these topics are not target language speakers, but in the spirit of "doing the best they can" will learn vocabulary related to music, art, sports, health or another special topic and will integrate it as much as possible in their classes. Also, these teachers learn bit by bit some of the commands they hear from other classroom teachers such as "Form a line," "Listen," and "Eyes to the front" and end up using these commands in the target language in their own classes.

Music and art in particular lend themselves very well to language instruction, even if the teacher does not speak the language. Often art teachers will focus on works by target language artists and will integrate the cultural aspects of the target culture art as much as possible. Music, again a language unto itself, is a gold mine of inspiration and input for language. Children learn and retain a great deal by singing in the target language. Fabulous music teachers make every attempt to integrate as much target language music as possible into their music curriculum. In addition, these teachers sometimes also integrate songs in several other languages into their music class. This effort enriches the students from both a language and cultural standpoint. The value of music and art in providing increased cultural input cannot be overstated.

> *"I feel the combination of language and music helped them to become much better, more creative thinkers and problem solvers."*
> *– Deb H, Language Immersion Parent*

> *"It is SO rewarding to teach these elementary immersion students, for many reasons, but this is an experience that delights me every time: The kids are singing in about 10 languages in their upcoming program. I have found that most of these languages use an imploded 't' sound. All I have to do is explain the difference and model it once, and they've got it. WIN!"* – *Kathleen P, Language Immersion Music Educator and Parent*

Music, art and physical education are often integrated into the regular classroom for part of the school day as well. When I taught in the elementary grades, my teaching teams always integrated all three of these subject areas regularly into the standards we were teaching. Many teachers use physical games to tap those kinesthetic learners when practicing reading or math skills. Often teachers integrate music into learning other subject skills as well. I was always fortunate to have teaching team members who were also interested in integrating art into the curriculum and had great joy in teaching the art of Matisse, Kandinsky, Chagall, Picasso, Dalí, Miró, and others. These were integrated into our language arts and social studies units and engaged students more thoroughly into the study of our basic curriculum. Students say they still have a great interest in art due to lessons from those early immersion years. I also hear regularly from students who tell me they still know all the words to a particular song from elementary school such as "Las posadas," "África," "Había una vez," or whichever song "stuck" after several years of learning hundreds of songs. This reveals the lasting power of capitalizing on a particular student's learning style and interest in a topic!

A researcher from the University of Minnesota once visited my classroom wanting to interview students in English for a research study. I declined, insisting that he interview my students in Spanish. He disagreed, believing they did not have the language skills to express ideas effectively. I argued in defense of my students, responding, "Then you aren't asking the right questions." He countered that they would not have the depth of vocabulary to talk about their feelings or abstract topics. I asked him to step into my third grade classroom to observe the discussion we were about to have on the art of Picasso. During that discussion students talked about the intricacies of Picasso's various art periods.

One student commented on how some of Picasso's paintings showed "naked" women. Though we weren't looking at nude paintings (it was third grade, after all), I acknowledged that this was true. Eric, a normally quiet, subdued boy in the classroom, jumped in to explain to his peers how in Picasso's art nude subjects weren't "naughty." He claimed they were simply forms to show how the human body is a piece of art, and that we should all look at it respectfully and not laugh. He went on to explain that Picasso revealed new ways of looking at the human body and it was an important contribution to art. Needless to say, the researcher was amazed by the student's ability to discuss the intricacies of art and social behavior with such depth of language skill and vocabulary. He then agreed that quite possibly my students did not need to be interviewed in English. As their teacher, I was relieved they had risen to the occasion and was extremely proud of their abilities once again.

Immersion Students Compared to Native-Speaking Students

Researchers have identified some equality in skills between immersion students and native speakers as early as second grade, and more so by fifth grade, in the areas of reading and listening. However, immersion students do not compare to native students in the productive areas of speaking and writing. They have communicative competence but operate with less complex grammatical forms, using simpler patterns that are familiar to them in their first language (Swain 1984). To parents, this means that your child will gain some of the same skills gained by a native speaking child of the target language, primarily the *receptive* skills of reading and listening, where information is coming *in*. Your child will gain competence in the target language but will not become native-like in the *productive* skills of speaking or writing, where information is going *out*. They will gain great skills in communication, however, and will be able to express their thoughts in a manner that is understandable by native speakers. An example is the following note, written to the school music teacher by a third grade student.

> "*Querida Sra. Pool, Gracias para todo como, coro, música, programa de talento, el programa, y mucho más. Tu eres uno de mis favoritos maestras en todo el mundo y esto es un rason porque no quiero mover a un otro escuela después de cuarto grado. Yo deseo que tengas un verano muy bien y otra vez gracias para todo. Con cariño,*" – Language Immersion Student

If you read Spanish, you will see that errors are present in this note. These are errors that a native speaking student may or may not make. There is no doubt however, that a native speaker would be able to read and understand this note in spite of errors such as word choice, masculine/feminine agreement, or inappropriate use of the familiar verb form, usage that appears commonly with young immersion students. The language is accurate enough that it is highly understandable and even uses some higher-level grammar, such as the subjunctive. It is quite possible that a native speaking third grade student might make some of the same errors found in this writing sample as well. If you do not read Spanish, you should be able to tell that it is a note to a teacher, using complete sentences, and expressing a string of connected thoughts. This alone is cause for celebration.

It is part of immersion magic that children develop the ability to function with competence when communicating with native speakers. They are able to express their ideas even though they are not like a native speaker in their production. Though some immersion students have scored in the "heritage speaker" range on college placement tests, not all students will score at that range. As with any academic skill, an individual's persistence, interest, and continued practice will create huge differences in outcomes. One former student expressed a more typical self-evaluation of her language competence, noting that she did not reach the level of a native speaker, "I can't speak at the speed of native speakers and I have an accent." This doesn't mean that she doesn't speak the language well; it just means that it is not native-like.

Immersion students will make errors just as they sometimes do in their first language, but they will have skills far beyond what they could ever achieve by beginning language study in high school. Again, it all comes back to time. With time and education, immersion students' skills will improve but they will always remain a native speaker of English, not the target language, unless they have the good fortune to either live in a bilingual family, a community, or a country where the language of immersion is spoken.

"I am a visual learner so the Spanish language was naturally easier for me. It seemed to logically make more sense to me. I wasn't as confident in my English reading and writing. However, I don't believe it would have been any better in a non-immersion school."
– Annie P, Former Language Immersion Student

> *"It is always amazing to hear my children speak with native speakers and be able to communicate their thoughts without any inhibitions."* – Language Immersion Parent

The majority of immersion students reflecting on their language competency feel very good about their skills. Nearly every student responding to questions about their language abilities noted that they have retained very good skills and continue to use the language often. A full 89% of student survey respondents indicated that they have used their Spanish skills in work or social settings since leaving the immersion program. Many have used the target language to work in health clinics and hospitals, in retail, customer service, human relations, banks, courtrooms, churches, schools, and therapy centers. They have also provided a wide range of interpreting services in many other types of work settings. While they do not claim native language competency most note that their immersion language skills continue to serve them well.

> *"I reached a level of competency that satisfied me. I was able to pass my college Language Proficiency Exam and skip four years of University language courses."* – Shawna V, Former Language Immersion Student

> *"I'll never be as good at Spanish as I'd like, just because it's so hard to maintain a language without truly practicing and finding people to help you keep learning. But I am satisfied with the depth of my knowledge, especially compared to non-immersion programs."* – Janet G-M, Former Language Immersion Student

> *"I don't know how competent they actually became but when they hear Spanish on TV or at a movie or in a song they have no problems understanding what is being said. They are completely able to function in a Spanish speaking country."* – Anne J, Language Immersion Parent

Watching Your Child Grow

The elementary school years are magical because you watch your child change from a very young, relatively dependent kindergartener into a fairly independent pre-adolescent with strong opinions. The growth from a little human being into a fifth grader you barely recognize is truly a wonder to observe. The physical growth, as well as the social and academic development, is stunning. You are an integral part of this process and yet in many ways you are an outsider witnessing a wonder of nature that happens with or without your involvement. How much better to be involved and supportive and a big part of the fun!

Though extensive growth is happening, I will note that the recurring theme of concern from parents about their child and the language immersion experience sort of rises and falls like a wave in the ocean. There are times of great success and growth and times of rest and regeneration. Try to look at the low, slow times as a natural part of the process rather than becoming worried that the pace of moving ahead isn't always constant. When your child goes through a period where English skills lag a bit behind that of English-only peers, celebrate the things that are growing. Relax, and know that everything will work out all right. Your child is a native speaker of English and will work out the intricacies of the language long before they head off to college or even high school.

I return again to Weise's "First Grade Freak-Out" (2014) in which she comments:

> Okay, I've exaggerated a bit here. The freak-out is usually more of a slow build. But at some point in every parent's... immersion journey, it really hits home that students in all-English classrooms *spend more time learning English*. And it shows in their work. The question you need to ask yourself is: how much of a problem is this? And the answer, *all* the research shows, is not much. But *only* if you look at how students do over time.

Enjoy the growth through the elementary immersion grades. It is a joy. It is exciting. It represents some of the more memorable times you will have with your child before they leave home for college. Be there. Be engaged. But also relax and let the "gift" you gave your child grow in the way that all those years of immersion research have shown repeatedly that it will. Be reassured that everything will indeed be ok.

> *"All's well. They learned. They flourished. They're adults and college grads now, both proficient in Spanish." – Barb N-M, Language Immersion Parent*

CHAPTER 5
The Struggling Learner in an Immersion Setting

Michael was a diligent student who tried his best and worked hard. He had an extremely supportive family who really wanted Michael to succeed. It was evident early on, however, that Michael was struggling to keep up with his peers. His mother would often sit in parent conference meetings in tears because she wanted so much for everything to be easier and for Michael's learning difficulties to disappear.

Michael's family briefly considered the possibility of an English-only program, but their desire for him to learn a second language, and their faith that it truly was the best possible option they could give their son, made them continue to choose immersion each year for his education. In addition, Michael had several siblings in the immersion program who were succeeding, so the family was fully invested in the language immersion life. Michael continued to struggle throughout his elementary educational experience, but each year made slight gains until he caught up by middle school and found school less challenging.

As an adult, Michael doesn't really recall having difficulties in school, and in fact notes that high school was easy for him. He mostly recalls that he was always "really good at math." In fact, he always received good grades in math. Michael went on to university and graduate school and eventually received a Master's degree in Mechanical Engineering. He took Spanish in college because he enjoyed it and thought it was fun. He was a Spanish interpreter for a hospital for two years prior to receiving an engineering job for a medical device company.

Would Michael have been as successful had the immersion process not engaged his brain so fully that he could complete very difficult graduate studies later in life? We will never know for sure how immersion contributed to his brain development, but it does not seem to have limited his education in the long run and may have contributed to his success later in life. In reflecting on his immersion experience he noted, "The Spanish Immersion program had a great impact on my life. It has made me more culturally aware, helped me meet new people and opened new opportunities that I would not have otherwise had. I'm regularly surprised how often I use this skill either at work or socially."

Michael is an example of how early struggles in elementary school teach one to use several strategies to compensate for learning difficulties. These strategies can be utilized throughout the school experience, in post-secondary education and in future employment to help one achieve wonderful things. This story also reveals how families and teachers can contribute to a child's positive self-esteem. My memories are of how this great kid struggled. His memories, however, are all positive and he recalls little of the struggle. His parents obviously did a great job continually letting him know he was a capable learner.

Language immersion schools usually have the same percentages of students who struggle as other schools in their home school district. Elementary immersion teachers, like any public school teachers, will effectively teach ALL students including those with dyslexia, attention-deficit disorders, hearing, speech and visual challenges, and any number of other learning differences (Lipton,

1998). Academic difficulties are rarely caused by the language being learned but by processing skills, learning delays or any disabilities or challenges that would be present in an English-only school as well. Students needing additional assistance range from those with simple confusion to those with major learning impairments. The vast majority completes their language learning education and goes on to successful college experiences and great employment opportunities. Many aren't true struggling learners but merely face a few challenges and need to work through how to process information as efficiently as possible for their individual learning styles.

> *"Language Immersion taught me many things, one of those being to never give up. I faced many challenges, but I was able to get through it. Immersion helped me build a stronger sense of myself.... I wanted to drop out every year and be in normal classes like all my other friends, but my parents didn't let me give up. I thank them for making me stick through it because I think that being fluent in Spanish is part of my identity."*
> *– Former Language Immersion Student*

A child who faces challenges in school presents a hurdle for every parent. Once again, parental concerns are heightened when you choose your child's educational experience to occur in a second language. Irene Brouwer Konyndyk in her book *Foreign Languages for Everyone* (2011) states:

> Certainly learning another language is hard work in and of itself . . . But I've learned that it's entirely possible to successfully teach struggling students another language . . . I believe that all students should be given the opportunity to learn a foreign language. I also believe that, especially in a multicultural world, these students deserve teachers and materials that can help them through their individual difficulties.

She discusses the fact that these very students are often highly inventive, with amazing strengths and talents. The joy of education is solving the puzzle and finding the keys that lead to their success in the typical educational system. Struggling immersion students benefit from the very nature of this type of program as language immersion tends to engage a style of teaching that actually taps into the strengths of these students, such as auditory or kinesthetic learning styles. This helps them develop strategies for learning that they will use throughout their educational lives.

A survey given to language immersion professionals by researchers at the University of Minnesota, Fortune and Menke (2009), revealed that the seven most frequent issues of immersion learners are:

1. Reading Comprehension
2. Basic Reading Skills
3. Attention Deficit Hyperactivity Disorder (ADHD)
4. Listening Comprehension
5. Speech or Language Impairment
6. Oral Expression
7. Math Reasoning and Calculation

These issues fall very close to what would be found in a school where your child would be learning in English as well. All are part of the list of disabilities identified in the Individuals with Disabilities Education Act of 2004 (IDEA). This act applies to all students, regardless of educational program.

Fortunately, language immersion teachers employ methods that are highly beneficial to students with any of the above concerns. Even more so than traditional elementary teachers, immersion teachers use lots of examples, act out what they are teaching, use whole-body kinesthetic activities, incorporate music and games to teach lessons, use a wide variety of visuals to help explain concepts, and rely naturally on lots of repetition as part of their teaching.

Language immersion teachers also teach to every type of learning style a student may have to make sure the lesson is understood in the second language. In addition, teachers differentiate instruction for both content and language to be sure it is accessible to all learners. They make changes as needed to subject matter to make it more comprehensible, by breaking it down into manageable chunks, re-stating lessons in different ways, or providing challenge opportunities to students who have already mastered the material. While all the methods listed above are common in all elementary schools, immersion teachers, because they are teaching in a language that is not the child's home language, must exaggerate these methods and utilize these techniques to their fullest. Language immersion instruction by design provides a naturally rich environment for all students, but especially for students who struggle.

Immersion teachers also encourage risk taking and allow students to make errors without fear. While all teachers are trained in the benefits of an error-correction-free classroom, immersion teachers at all levels are most likely to implement the ideal. Zachmeir-Ruh (2005) states that "the development of a respectful, caring community in which all children feel valued and in which making mistakes is an accepted part of the learning process is a primary goal." Even though immersion classrooms are natural environments for a rich and encouraging experience, and mistakes are accepted freely, some students will still struggle and need additional support through the many resources available in schools. Most often, teachers will start with additional interventions in the classroom and other help will be added as needed and determined by the school staff in consultation with you, the parent.

Jessica was a young learner who had tremendous difficulties in school. She received a great deal of additional support from teachers, special education specialists, school psychologists, and other building staff. She was a non-reader when she finished first grade, and when she reached fifth grade she was still reading at a level with simple pattern sentences such as "The cat wore a hat as it sat near the bat." She read at the same level in both English and Spanish. On the other hand, Jessica had excellent listening comprehension and spoke fluently in Spanish. She understood everything in school that was presented orally. Her difficulties were in reading and writing in both languages.

Jessica's parents were always very supportive of her and though they struggled with Jessica's difficulties in school, they never considered taking her out of the program. They simply continued to support her as she struggled throughout her educational experience. When Jessica graduated from high school, she had the same level of English reading and writing skills she would have had in the English-only school, except that she was highly employable because she could understand and speak Spanish fluently. She found success in a career that emphasized telephone work in Spanish, a job that she would not have obtained had her educational experience only been in English.

Presenting research at a 2012 conference held by the Center for Research in Language Acquisition (CARLA), Dr. Fred Genesee, of McGill University in Montreal, noted that students with low levels of general ability are at risk for low achievement in any school program, but are *not* at greater risk in an immersion program. He also noted that minority students from low socio-economic households, while often being at risk in any school program, are *not* at greater risk in an immersion program. There is sometimes the view that children who have language impairment would jeopardize their English development because the target language is burdening their learning. Genesee presents the alternative view that children with language impairment have difficulty learning any language, and their difficulties in English are the same whether they learn two languages or only one language.

It was suggested by Dr. Genesee that immersion students are not at a greater risk for reading impairment but that they are instead at greater risk of receiving delayed support. He contends that the "wait and see" approach, or waiting to see if the target language is interfering, is not ideal. His research suggests that indicators of reading difficulties in early kindergarten are "reasonable" predictors, but that the spring of kindergarten provides even better at-risk indicators and that this data is quite accurate in predicting risk up to 2-3 years later (Genesee 2012). So while struggling learners are not at greater risk in immersion programs than in English-only programs, early identification and support provided as soon as possible is wise.

Getting Help for Your Child

Parents of struggling learners are constantly second guessing themselves and their decision to place their child in an immersion program. Some ask, "Wouldn't this be easier for my child if she was in an English program?" when really they mean, "Wouldn't this be easier for *our family* in an English-only program?" And indeed, the struggling student places extra challenges on the time, energy and patience of everyone in the family. Other families second-guess themselves because they are genuinely concerned with their child's progress and wonder if they have put them in the best environment for success. This is especially true when they see grades as determinants of future opportunities. They worry about their kids having lower self-esteem when they accomplish less than their peers.

When a child struggles, the main thing you can do is assure the child of your love, support, and pride in their accomplishments. Your child's anxiety level in school can be a reflection of your anxiety as a parent. You unknowingly may be placing additional stress on your child. As hard as this is, try to be as relaxed as you can and have faith in the process. You need to return to your reasons for choosing this program and recall that many of the "perks" of the program go way beyond simply learning to speak another language, but also include brain development and flexibility in thinking.

There are still those who believe that the ability to acquire a second language is a special talent that some people have and some do not. I do not subscribe to this belief. In fact, in early childhood education I have noticed that learning in a second language often evens the playing field. Though all students do not come into school with the same skills and abilities, they all come in for the most part with minimal experience in the target language and start at the same point. Though they may process information differently and at varying rates, they are all assimilating this new input at the same time. They are at the same point, at this one moment in time, in this one skill area. Children with disabilities frequently shine at the verbal part of language learning, the cornerstone of kindergarten instruction, and may even outperform some of their more academically talented classmates. This may be due to experiencing a growth of confidence in the immersion classroom. It may be because teachers assume all students do not understand as quickly in the second language and therefore tend to repeat directions, review main points, act out the meaning of things, and use exaggerated facial expressions and gestures to make meaning clear. Or, it may be that this is just a bit of magic that motivates, excites, and delights these children.

Even though children may thrive in the beginning, if learning issues are present, they will emerge at some point and need additional attention. It is not uncommon for learning struggles to appear once the written part of language begins to have a more dominate presence in the school day. The right evaluation process, additional support for those areas identified for remediation, and extra time allowed to complete work and assessments often help these students be every bit as successful as their peers in the long run. Getting to "the long run" is the hard part for many parents. It is natural for parents to focus on the difficulties which may occur in reading and writing rather than celebrating the aspects that are going well, such as listening, speaking and gaining content (in math, science, etc.). This is where school staff can help. They will have a comprehensive procedure in place to determine where they can help, how as parents you can help, and how all of you can celebrate the positives.

Elementary programs are constantly evaluating the progress of their students. Be assured that your child is being monitored, and you will be informed if any type of intervention or assistance is determined to be of value in your child's case. Most assistance will come in the form of extra time and extra help right in the classroom. You may be asked to reinforce learning with additional practice at home. The best assistance you can provide early on is to keep reading, reading, and reading some more with your child. Go to the library and make sure there is a constant rotation of 10 or more books in your home at all times. If your child only wants to read via technology, use that as a reward after you have spent 15 minutes reading hard print books together. Any additional work you can provide at home will only help your child, especially as resources in our public schools continue to dwindle. Think of the time working with your child as one of the tools in the resource box to help your child be successful.

Most schools now use early intervention strategies in a variety of formats to provide assistance in the early grades. While your child is in the kindergarten and first grade years, where a high percentage of time is spent in the target language, you still are acting on a great amount of faith that all of this is going to work. Once your child enters second grade and starts having lessons in English, you and the school will both have more information about whether additional intervention is necessary, or if your child just needs extra time to reach peak learning ability.

The process for assisting struggling students varies from state to state as well as from school to school. The process may also vary in private or charter schools that sometimes follow different guidelines than public schools. A general overview of what may happen is as follows: A teacher begins to notice low classroom performance and discusses concerns with you, the parent. The teacher may then outline what he or she will do to assist in the classroom, and what you can do at home as parents to help your child. You may be asked to practice with flashcards, spend time reading together, practice math skills, write sentences, play learning games or try many other learning activities and report back to the teacher. A few weeks may pass to see if these interventions help your child succeed. If not, you and the teacher will meet to discuss additional strategies to try, and you will probably wait a few more weeks to see if these new techniques are working.

Meanwhile the teacher is most likely reporting to a building team regarding your child's struggles. Most schools have an internal process where a team of professionals meets to discuss students who are struggling and offers suggestions and support. This usually involves the teacher, an administrator, and special education professionals, such as a social worker, school psychologist, learning specialist, speech pathologist, or other special needs teachers. As a team they will problem solve to see if new ideas or suggestions may be helpful to the teacher in working with your child in the classroom. Later on, if the strategies used by you and the teacher working together are not producing the desired effect, the teacher will return to this team to request additional assistance. Observation and evaluation may follow to determine if your child qualifies for additional support services. The criteria used as qualification for special services is usually determined by the school district and/or state; your school professionals will follow these guidelines. You will be notified along the way of any assessment or evaluation and also of any results found. At this time, the team will determine if your child is experiencing a developmental delay or has a learning disability or information-processing condition (Woelber 2004).

If a genuine learning delay or disorder is found to exist through the trial of several interventions as well as assessments, you will find that immersion programs, like any elementary school, will offer support services. Sometimes this comes in the form of additional assistance in the classroom via instructional aides or assistants. At times small groups may be utilized either in the classroom, in a nearby location outside the classroom, or in a separate classroom. These periods usually occur for a short time daily or a few times a week. Special education teachers or instructional aides use techniques such as multisensory input (auditory, visual, kinesthetic), oral and written practice, and flashcards, to name a few. The strategies and techniques employed by teachers continue to amaze me with their creativity as well as their demonstrated success at helping each child improve academic skills.

> *"Students who struggle in the first language will struggle in the second language. A struggling learner in English is not caused by their immersion education. In some cases, learning to read in Spanish that is so phonetic can be helpful for some students that struggle with reading. If a parent does have a student that struggles, open communication should happen between the parents and the teacher in order to better accommodate the student's needs. Be an informed parent about the services the school/district can provide." – Language Immersion Educator*

In my own experience, any interventions in the kindergarten year were generally contained in the classroom and administered by the teacher It really does take a trial period to determine if a student just needs a bit of extra time to mature, needs extra learning time, or actually has a learning concern that needs to be addressed. This is true, especially given the age range of students in a single grade, which can vary by 12 months or more. The kindergarten year is a great time to allow the child to develop. It also gives the teacher time to try various strategies in the classroom with the hope of identifying a bit of magic that helps the student learn more easily.

In one immersion school, all first grade students were given reading assessments, and any student who needed an extra boost was given time with an aide weekly to work on vocabulary and practice reading. These one-on-one extra minutes helped numerous students get over learning hurdles right away, until they no longer required extra assistance. Some students were in the program for a few weeks and others remained in it all year. It was a successful way to ensure that all students were ready for second grade, where more independent reading is encouraged. Programs such as this are common in many schools, though the model will vary significantly with each one.

Another immersion school had a highly successful peer-tutoring program in place. At first, parents may doubt that peer tutoring can be of benefit. Nothing could be further from the truth! "Students teaching students" is a very robust model and proves to be highly beneficial for both the tutor and tutee. Data collected over the years points to numerous students receiving exactly the extra help needed in just 15 minutes a day. The peer-tutoring program was highly structured with every five minutes dedicated to a particular task. It featured lots of data notation by tutors, constant monitoring by teachers to ensure on-task behaviors, positive encouragement by tutors and teachers, and effective use of time. Many students became "graduates" of peer tutoring and needed no further learning assistance, never needed special education services, and had very positive self-esteem from being in the program. Student tutors received great benefits as well. They learned data-keeping skills and strategies for being positive and encouraging. Tutors also increased in self-esteem and self-confidence while working in the peer-tutoring program. It is wonderful to witness the satisfaction of tutors when their tutees achieve success.

Programs such as the two described above are creative and original. I witnessed great successes from both programs, with students reaching grade level reading skills and avoiding the need for support services on a formal plan. You may find something similar in your school. Allow the school to try out different programs to help your child. Everyone has your child's best interest at heart and wants your child to succeed. If one program or intervention doesn't work, the school will try something else. You as a parent can always advocate for your child to try something new as well. I can't emphasize enough how important it is to talk regularly with the teacher and others helping your child at school. Consistent communication is the key to working as a team for student success.

> *"You know your child. Listen to your child. If he or she is having a lot of emotional difficulty/academic difficulty, bring it up to the teacher. Work together to figure out the best path and strategies for your child. Listen to each other. You are a team." – Laura M, Language Immersion Educator*

Parents also should be prepared to offer additional assistance at home. Some parents opt for additional tutoring in the home language outside of school to supplement the work that is being done in school. It is tempting to look for a quick fix, so your child can catch up as soon as possible. Sometimes problems can be solved very quickly. Other times the very nature of the child's struggle is that they have a developmental delay and simply need more time to catch up. In any case, remember that your child is just that—a child—and has plenty of time to succeed. Do not add to your child's stress by showing a high level of anxiety. Offer love and positive strokes and your child will reward you by doing their very best.

Staying in Immersion vs. Leaving

I realize how hard it is for parents to make decisions about an educational setting and whether or not to keep plugging away at second language learning or just make life easier and go to an English-only program. Research results show that learning-disabled students enrolled in dual language immersion schools in Virginia, when compared with English-only students, did not perform differently on standardized tests of academic content (Myers 2011). The children in this study had equal opportunity to succeed no matter which program they were enrolled in, the exception being that those students in the immersion program also gained a second language. Dr. Myers indicates that the data of this study show that immersion is an appropriate environment for students identified with special education needs.

> Students do not need to be moved to a monolingual English program simply because of a disability classification. They can enter TWI (two-way immersion) programs and succeed in them while reaping the benefits of an enriched education offered in two languages....If on the surface it appears that all things are equal, they are not really equal: the TWI students speak, read and write in two languages. TWI students leave school with more. They leave with two languages.

In another research study, students in Grades 1 to 3 in a French immersion program were compared to students in an English-only program. Growth in reading skill outcomes occurred for all students, with the immersion students achieving higher scores and faster growth than the English-only students (Kruk and Reynolds 2012). Burnett (1990) noted that immersion does not cause learning disabilities, and that switching from an immersion program is inadvisable due to the negative impact this has on the child's self-esteem.

French immersion kindergarten children were tested and then re-tested in first grade, with results indicating that children with language disabilities were benefitting from learning in a French immersion program. Psychologist Margaret Bruck has collected large amounts of data supporting her contention that language disabled children can acquire proficiency in the French language while continuing to develop skills in their own language. They also learn reading and math concepts even though they are taught in French. It may take these children longer than their peers to learn the material but they do succeed. Bruck also has observed that language disabled children often do not succeed in a typical French-as-a-second-language program but that the French immersion program provides a "more suitable and natural environment for these children to learn French" (Bruck 1978). She continues, "Immersion does not cause or compound problems: children who have problems in immersion programs would have the same constellation of problems were they in an English class." In further study, French immersion students who transferred to an English program because of academic difficulties were assessed after their first year of English education. The results showed that their cognitive, academic, linguistic and social psychological status compared equally with their peers with academic difficulty that remained in the immersion program (Bruck 1985). This suggests again that the immersion program was not harming the education of these students but that other cognitive factors were at play. Those who remained in the program, however, continued to gain second language skills.

Learners who struggle with other issues still understand as much of the immersion language and perform as well as above-average students on tests of communication skills.. In addition, struggling learners rated as high as above-average students on every measure of oral production: grammar, pronunciation, vocabulary and fluency of communication. This indicates that below-average students benefit from immersion education as much as any student. On English tests, struggling students were no further behind than struggling students in English-only programs (Swain 1984). Ability does not play a more significant role in immersion programs than regular school programs. A child will do just as well, though struggling, as they would do in any school. And, as stated previously, when allowed to respond orally, students may do as well as their peers who are highly successful in school. Immersion, lending itself to oral production, may be of great benefit to these students, and overall should not cause any detriment to their education, even in the nonverbal areas of academic learning.

Even with research and examples about the general success of these learners in immersion schools, it is difficult for parents to simply wait and trust that there will also be a success story for their child. This is understandable. Your child is your most important concern right now, in this program, at this age. It is difficult to trust the experience of others, and transferring to an English-only school presents an immediate solution, if not the best solution long term. The assurance parents may feel, knowing they will be able to better assist their child because they can understand home and school work themselves is powerful. My years of experience with struggling students sometimes led to tear-filled sessions at the conference room table with parents, now struggling themselves with the question, "Do we go or do we stay?"

The few students I've known who transferred to an English-only program continued to struggle and need additional support. Basically, the educational process is the same, but the child is not gaining the second language skill that could make them more employable later in life. The additional brain flexibility and development is also being lost. Of course, transferring to an English language program generally relieves parent anxiety and guilt and therefore can provide relief to the child as well. I've seen several cases of "If Dad's happy, everyone is happy." Of course, the same stress relief goes for Mom as well. Once parents feel they have taken positive action for their child, they become less stressed, thus making the family dynamic happier.

Troy struggled every year throughout school as well. Troy worked hard, engaged fully in school and had a supportive family. Each year after third grade, however, Troy's family made the decision to pull him from the immersion program and enroll him in an English-only school in the district the following fall. Every year we would have a goodbye party for Troy, but every September we would find him back in our school. He would be so upset each summer about going to a different school and missing his friends that his parents would relent and allow him to return. His peers would be so happy to see him return and he would engage fully in school again. Troy continued to struggle, though he received many forms of support through special services, teachers, and educational aides.

Troy's parents were very pleased with his success as he continued making gains and was less behind at the start of each school year than the year before. Strategies he learned in elementary school for getting work done, listening well even when he didn't fully understand, and making study adjustments, served him well in his classes in middle school and high school.

Families who hang in there and make it work are always glad they did. The story of Michael from the beginning of this chapter, as well as the stories of Jessica and Troy, are examples of students and families who stuck it out, and reaped the benefits. It's as if all the early struggles really pay off when students go to middle and high school where most of the school day is in English. Students learn strategies through struggling in language immersion that can be utilized in all their classes, helping them succeed.

"For my first child, no issues. He was advanced. My second son was testing as a "non-reader." With the assistance of aides and one-on-one help he was caught up and on the (state test) was a near perfect score in reading." – Language Immersion Parent

"Two of my three were "low" English readers in K-6. Not likely due to Spanish, but as a parent you always wonder. They had extra resources that helped them and they were at grade level by 4th to 6th grade. Their reading and writing has been on track throughout." – Language Immersion Parent

A parent of an immersion student with dyslexia describes her family's experience, which began with a clinician stating, "You've got to get her out of that school." She shares her thoughts:

> Susan was already in a good learning environment . . . Her teacher was aware of her needs and my daughter received extra help with math. She was given smaller pieces to memorize for the reading and writing assignments . . . She was given five spelling words instead of ten . . . In third grade, Susan started after-school private tutoring for reading . . . The more I read, the more I realized that there was no right answer, but this might be Susan's one chance to learn a second language. I could find no conclusive studies showing immersion was harmful. By the end of fifth grade, Susan's reading scores had started to approach average grade levels and she had started staying up late at night reading in her bed! . . . Each year we have made the decision that this is the right place for her. We have been lucky to have responsive teachers who are willing to adapt the curriculum to something more manageable for our daughter. She has found a way to succeed in school and to get her homework done on time. We feel that this has been the best school choice for her. (Anton 2004)

Another parent writes:

> "My son went into second grade at a kindergarten reading level. He was identified for a reading intervention in English with the reading teacher. We took him to a psychologist where he was diagnosed with ADHD...We continued to read with him at home on a regular basis and by the end of second grade he was in the top reading group for his class. Just because your student struggles, doesn't mean they always will. Don't give up. Do all that you can to support your child. The school can only do so much. Don't be afraid to seek help. You are your child's best advocate and the sooner they receive an intervention the better their chances of catching up."
> – Jeanne S, Language Immersion Parent and Educator

For parents of struggling children the key, once again, is to be proactive. Talk early on with the teacher, your partner in helping your child succeed. Most often, early intervention by the teacher is all that is necessary. The teacher may solicit the assistance of teaching aides or assistants who can offer additional small group or one-on-one time with your child. If necessary, make an appointment with an administrator. Do what is needed to get the help your child needs.

> "Support must be provided in the second language for struggling learners. Many parents want to blame immersion for their child's struggles but the reality is struggling learners would struggle in the native language also. The difference is that immersion can actually help with cognitive benefits in the long run." – Patrick S, Language Immersion Educator

Immersion researcher Fred Genesee encourages the early identification of at-risk students, as well as early interventions for them. He also notes that immersion programs do not cause difficulties in language and literacy; rather, these concerns are similar to those in English-only programs. The interventions that work in English programs are the very same interventions that will be effective in immersion programs (Gouin 2009).

Researchers in a Canadian French immersion program studied the effects of early identification and intervention of at-risk students in a grade 1 classroom. Basing their work on research that recognizes the cross-language transfer of reading skills, the early intervention program had a considerable impact on the reading development of the identified struggling students. Students' skills nearly reached grade level reading skill after a 20-week intervention. The French reading achievement levels were significantly higher than that of the group who did not receive early intervention. In addition to improvement of their actual reading scores, their percentile scores improved as well, suggesting they made more progress during the same time period than their peers.

> In sum, our research demonstrates that supplemental instruction of sufficient duration and intensity for those who may be at-risk for later reading difficulties, provided early in their educational careers in small group settings, may be the key to breaking the cycle of failure . . . It is possible that with appropriate support, these students will become fluent, proficient readers in French and English. (Wise and Chen 2010)

Another study by these same researchers looked at another intervention type, supplemental reading in small groups with phonological awareness training and letter-sound instruction twice a week for 18 weeks. Again, students had significant gains and maintained those gains for the remaining two years of the study (Wise, D'Angelo and Chen 2016.) This research indicates that interventions can be effective in addressing deficits and help students with reading development.

Immersion teachers and support staff use many different types of interventions, such as giving students extra time, reduction of required assignments, repetition, or small group and individual practice. These interventions are indeed the very same as in an English program, just delivered in the second language. Again, I stress that the techniques employed by immersion teachers, including acting out instructions and ideas, and using multiple means of presenting content—teaching strategies which are aimed at helping young children understand something in a second language—also are effective strategies for struggling learners. The language itself is not the barrier. Other learning difficulties are in play, difficulties that would be present regardless of receiving instruction in the first or second language. Fortunately, immersion teachers are highly talented in helping struggling students succeed in school.

> *"My son was slow to read in Spanish. His first grade teacher, Sra. P, made tapes for him to listen to while we looked at books. Then, the summer between first and second grades, his brain clicked and he was ready to learn to read in English and Spanish." – Sandra S, Language Immersion Parent*

As a parent, you can advocate for your child and work with the team at the immersion school to be sure your child receives the help needed early on in their education. Remember that you are also part of that team, and extra effort will be needed from you to provide additional support and practice for your child.

> *"Keep at it. Focus on the Positive. Celebrate successes. Don't compare your child to another." – Brynn L, Language Immersion Teacher*

> *"Our daughter struggled with both math and learning to read. We questioned our decision at that point on some level, but not*

enough to even consider withdrawing. Our thought was to ensure our daughter received resources." – Marla B, Language Immersion Parent

When You've Given It All You've Got

There have been occasions when I have helped parents make the difficult decision to choose an English-only program. This has been extremely rare. My gut response is always to keep children in the immersion program and to continue working on educational success. However, at times I have supported a parental decision to leave immersion. These rare instances have included the following situations:

1) *The family life has deteriorated enormously due to the stress of the language learning experience for the entire family.* Parents are frustrated to the point that their marriage or relationship with their child is clearly falling apart. The stress present in the family is so great that some sort of action is needed to try and save the quality of family life in the home. Often, there are other factors such as one or more parents not being fully on board with immersion education in the first place, other relatives applying pressure to make a different choice, siblings acting out in order to receive more attention, or any number of other issues affecting the family that are not related to language learning at all. Sometimes when this is the case, immersion education is the easiest factor to eliminate in order to stabilize the family and the childhood experience for the student.
2) *The self-esteem of the student has become so low due to lack of success or pressure from parents that emotional stability is in question.* If the child has lost the simple joy of being a child, it may be time to act. I always look at student attitudes in school. Are they happy in school? Do they have friends? Do they like to play?

It is important to evaluate whether it is just the academics, which can be supplemented and supported, or whether the entire school experience is a negative factor. A child's mental health should always be reviewed and supported. Only once in more than 30 years of education did I feel the need to support a parental decision to remove a student from immersion due to low self-esteem at a dangerous level.

3) *A student has been diagnosed with auditory learning disabilities.* In rare cases a student has an auditory processing impairment that causes severe problems in discerning differences in the target and native language and interferes with learning. Sometimes students overcome this disability but sometimes they do not. Though reluctantly, I have agreed with parents on certain occasions that English-only education might be easier for their child.

"If your child is a struggling learner, it doesn't mean you should necessarily take him/her out of the second language instruction. Your child will probably struggle in the first language as well and all people are capable of becoming bilingual. Being bilingual will be a big benefit in the long run and worth the effort." – Kathleen J, Language Immersion Educator

All in all, when a student struggles with learning, it poses a challenge for parents, but it is a challenge that can be overcome. Teamwork, communication, patience, and trust all come into play in leading the student to success. However, don't expect everything to be perfect. Your child will learn many important lessons from seeing life isn't always perfect and still working to achieve the best results possible. The lifelong skill of being able to face a challenge and learn from it, regardless of how the situation turns out, is invaluable. If parents can give the process time, the situation may resolve itself. If the problem persists, consider struggling along with your child to help them do their best and also gain the lifelong skill of being able to function in a second language. This skill will help boost them above others when it comes to secondary and post-secondary academics as well as employability.

> *"My daughter struggled in school in general so while not as proficient as most I'm thrilled she can converse with Spanish speaking people."* –Language Immersion Parent

CHAPTER 6
Homework, Projects and Presentations How Do I Help?

If you are competent in the language of the immersion school, you may have few concerns about your ability to understand assignments that come home from school with your child. Most parents of immersion students are not competent in the target language, however. The majority of my students' parents had never studied a language, or had studied in high school or college without attaining a high level of competence, or had lost any skills they once had. Due to lack of confidence or competence, parents are justifiably worried about helping their child in school.

Both initially and throughout the middle grades, a parent's biggest worry is about helping with schoolwork. Parents have listed language-related fears as their biggest concern about the immersion life: not being able to understand the teacher, not being able to help with homework, and not being able to read books in the target language. These fears are all related to parents though, not their children. Parents never stated that they were concerned their child wouldn't understand the language.

> *"Our family does not speak Spanish. It was intimidating to be at the school itself. I could not read any of the signage. I couldn't understand what the teachers and the children were saying."*
> *– Julie G, Language Immersion Parent.*

> *"Not being able to help them with their homework, because I don't speak the language, scared me." – Language Immersion Parent*

If thousands of children can take language risks every day, then I believe parents can too. Even though you may have fears about language, you should know that numerous parents just like you have navigated these waters successfully and come out on the other side with no regrets. The very first day is the time to jump in and face your fears about language. You would expect no less from your child.

So how do you help your child when you can't read the language? The answer yet again is simply to be supportive. Your child's teacher does not expect you to know the target language. In the early grades, teachers often are just starting to teach the "concept" of homework. This concept involves taking something home, doing it, and bringing it back to school. If a child can master the "take it home, bring it back" concept of homework, a huge skill is gained that will be utilized throughout their education. It takes some students a long time to learn this skill. I can't tell you how many times I've seen teachers help a student clean out a locker in search of missing homework only to find numerous completed assignments that had never been turned in. Parents and teachers teaming up early to ensure the skill of taking something home and returning it to school completed will help prevent the black hole of homework that can be found in school lockers.

As a parent, know that immersion homework issues are usually less frightening than they are imagined to be. Teachers are actually quite caring and their goal is for your child to be successful as well. Keep in mind that you are on the same team, rooting for your child to do their best. Teachers need your support mostly in providing a consistent environment for the student to complete assigned tasks. Generally your child will know exactly what to do on the homework assignment with no further explanation or assistance on your part. However, there is a great deal you can do as parents to assist your child:

- Establish a time commitment
- Manage target language homework
- Conquer organization
- Prioritize reading time and
- Gain perspective.

Establish a Time Commitment

Finding enough time for homework can be the biggest struggle parents face. In this overscheduled world, finding a regular study time in a consistent location is difficult at best. Many children are relegated to completing homework in the car, at a restaurant, or at a sibling's sports practice—hardly ideal settings for homework success. If you can master the consistent time and place requirement for homework, you will most likely succeed at this part of the language immersion experience. I encourage parents to keep a regular homework time five days a week, in a consistent place in the home. Even if your child has no homework that evening, it is best to insist that the time be observed by reading silently or doing some other educational activity like puzzles, word games or math games. This study and reading time should come before "screen time" if at all possible. I know of one family that implemented a "no screen" policy on school nights. This is becoming more and more difficult for families to enforce, but even limited screen-free times will be helpful in developing good study and reading habits in your children.

A rule of thumb often used in both immersion and traditional schools to determine an appropriate amount of time for homework is 10 minutes per grade in school. For example, 10 minutes in first grade, 20 minutes in second grade, 30 minutes in third grade and so on. I think it is reasonable to spend this amount of time every school night doing homework, educational activities or reading. As your child progresses through the school years, you will thank yourself for establishing this habit early. If your child knows they must sit in the "study area" and work on something educational during this time, they are more likely to develop the habit of bringing home the necessary work in order to get it out of the way. The "I don't have any homework" excuse will drift away over time if this habit is enforced consistently. It is also helpful if the study zone is in an area where parents can monitor and be engaged with the homework activity. Even if parents can't read the assignment, they can ask questions and show interest, which helps children stay on task and actually enjoy study time more.

Parents who enact a required study and reading time often get desirable results. Children learn that getting assignments done makes time go faster than just sitting and watching the clock. Don't be unreasonable in enforcing a lengthy study time, as young children should not sit terribly long working on homework. Follow the rule of thumb for time described earlier. If you find your child is spending a great deal more time than this, have a discussion with the teacher and work as a team to solve the problem. As a teacher, I often suggested that the parents of fifth grade students break the 50-minute homework block into 10-15 minute chunks, rather than one extended period. For some kids, this was magic. For others, parents and I had to brainstorm other solutions. Once your child knows that you and the teacher are communicating directly, it will greatly enhance the productivity you see during both school and home study time.

It is important that you evaluate any rewards you may be giving your child associated with this time. For example, if your child is rewarded with time on the computer when there is no homework, you will soon find that there is never any homework. Why do school work when playing on the computer or watching television seems infinitely more enjoyable? Be aware of what behavior you are rewarding and make changes if needed. Reward what you want to see! A child studying or reading for 20 minutes in second grade deserves a star on a chart and an end-of-week reward, such as a fun family activity, a special dinner choice on Friday, or whatever helps get the job done. As a former college professor said to me once, "You have to find out what each child's M&M is." What motivates your child? Maybe it really *is* an M&M, maybe it's playing outdoors, maybe it's getting a star on a chart, or maybe you are a really lucky parent and doing homework is super fun for your child. It is certainly worth your time to figure it out.

There has been a trend recently in some schools for a "no homework" policy. If this is the case in your school, you may still choose to hold a regular "study" time which can be replaced with reading together or doing family activities together. This is usually the goal of the no-homework movement—to allow children more time to be children and give families more quality time together. You could certainly use extra family time to engage in a language or cultural experience to reinforce the school day experience in a positive way.

Whether your school gives homework or not, be positive and keep supporting your child. I see advantages to both approaches. The extra family time and free "childhood time" of the no-homework movement is quite intriguing and has many merits. On the other hand, small and manageable homework assignments do prepare your child for the rigors of the educational experience they will encounter as they grow older. Good homework study habits created by young learners pay dividends in reduced stress over homework later on. Either way, be supportive and positive, and your child will be positive as well.

> *"I think they gained much more than just a second language. It taught them independence and responsibility for their learning (we were not able to help much with homework)." – Beth D, Language Immersion Parent*

Manage Target Language Homework

"I can't read the instructions!" is a common cry of language immersion parents. Of course, if the instructions are all in the target language it may be entirely true that you can't read them. But give it a try! See how much of it you can glean from what you read. You may surprise yourself. Your child learns by risk-taking and guessing all day long at school. This is a perfect time to be a positive role model and do some language risk-taking yourself.

When your child brings home a target language assignment remember that the teacher has explained it carefully to the class at least once, and more likely two or three times. Ask your child, "What did the teacher say you were supposed to do?" They probably know but aren't always willing to let *you* know that. Unfortunately, this is a game that language immersion students learn early on. If they pretend they don't understand what to do, they might get away with not doing it. Students learn the "language game" and play it well. If Mom or Dad can't read the assignment or doesn't know what to do, some children use this to their advantage and feign incomprehension as well. Sit down together and try to figure it out. Don't just look at the target language words and throw up your hands. Really take a good look at it and see if you can figure it out. This is a great way for students to develop perseverance and resilience.

When trying to work through homework instructions with their children, some parents invent their own games. One is the "silly assignment" game. Parents lead their child in a really goofy, silly direction and watch as their child leads them back. For example, if the assignment is to write a paragraph about a favorite hobby, the parent might say, "I think you are supposed to write about the lunchroom cook." The student will probably immediately correct the parent with "No, we're not. We are supposed to write about a hobby!" Children love to correct their parents.

You can always contact the teacher for further direction, but first you should be absolutely certain that your child does not understand what they need to do to complete the schoolwork. Come up with ways to work through the directions with your child. You may be surprised how fast your child understands what needs to be done if required to sit by your side as you painstakingly look up each word. Understanding sometimes magically reappears, just to be done with it and not have to wait for you to work through the directions. It won't take too many nights of spending this extra time for them to either stop pretending to not understand OR to pay attention better in class so they know what to do. Try the above suggestions, contact another parent for help, or have your child call a friend to try and find answers to your questions.

> *"Tell your child to do what they can. Even if it's wrong, the teacher may be able to see where the misunderstanding is occurring and address it—very likely a quick fix."* – Brynn L, Language Immersion Educator

> *"Don't help your kids too much. Let them struggle and fail once in awhile."* – Kathleen J, Language Immersion Educator

> *"Allow your child to make mistakes. It's part of the process."* – Language Immersion Educator

If you continue to struggle with homework instructions, have a chat with the teacher. You both have the same goal here, so team up! You can usually expect that teachers will send home special instructions in English to you if they really need you to help or if the task is complex. Many teachers keep up-to-date web pages with parent information and assignment explanations. Use the tools available to you. Translation apps allow you to take a photo of a homework page and then receive a translation. The quality of the translations from these apps is improving all the time and presents a great tool for parents. However, limit the use of translation apps to parents and do not have your child use it as a tool to translate and complete their homework. Do not suggest that your child use any electronic device to complete homework unless the teacher has given you instructions to do so. Lessons for using technology as a tool will occur in your school at some point, so watch for direction coming from either the teacher or an administrator in that respect. Remember, talking directly with the teacher is always, always, always important if your concerns and stress about homework are running high.

> *"Overall, I believe that my parents were most helpful because they were good communicators with my teachers, encouraged me if I was frustrated, but ultimately they believed in me and my ability to succeed."* – Allison M, Language Immersion Educator and Former Student

Don't worry about your own skills in knowing and understanding the target language. Sit down and let your child teach you what they are doing. Children love the role of being your teacher. If you read together and you say a word incorrectly, don't get upset. Your child will probably laugh at you and correct you. After laughing together you can carry on, and you will have learned something new.

As discussed in chapter three, I have found that many parents take language classes or try computer language learning when their child enters an immersion program. To this, I say hurrah! It is great if you want to learn the language too. You need to understand, however, that you will never keep up with your children. You can't be a child again, so you won't be the sponge for language that they are. As long as you go in knowing this, your own language learning can serve as a model for how important you think language learning is. That being said, it is not necessary for you to learn the target language for your child to be successful in language learning. Immersion works very well for children regardless of their parents' skill, or lack thereof, in the language.

> *"I think attending the immersion program was actually great for developing my independence because my parents don't speak Spanish. I had to be totally independent in completing assignments and homework since they couldn't understand any of it!" – Ellen T, Former Language Immersion Student*

> *"I think I learned to be more independent academically from an early age because my parents could not help me if I needed help. I would have to explain it in English and translate everything back to Spanish. Those are skills most students don't learn until high school, if at all." – Hannah C, Former Language Immersion Student*

> *"Immersion teachers take into consideration that most parents are not speakers of the target language and plan homework that can be done independently. Instead of helping their child with specific answers, parents should guide children by helping them think through the process. Focus on the skills needed to do the homework more, and less on the product." – Patrick S, Language Immersion Educator*

After English is introduced in second grade, you may find that more of the homework is in English. This is not because most of the day is now in English, but because teachers try to keep as much of the school day in the target language as possible. Teachers struggle with the need to squeeze all necessary subjects into the school day, especially when they are trying to do language arts in two languages. A solution is sometimes to send some of the English work home, which many parents also find is a relief—now it's easier to help and to read the instructions.

Another strategy that some immersion teachers have used to avoid the parent language comprehension issue is to send home math practice that doesn't involve a lot of language, particularly in the early grades. Parents can look at a math book and figure out the "language" of math, even if they don't know the words in the target language. You may find that some of your child's teachers utilize this technique as well. You should know that math becomes much more language-intense after fourth grade, making it more difficult for parents to assist with ease. You've heard it before—team up with your child's teacher and keep those communication channels open!

Another extremely useful technique is to establish a calling, texting, Facebook, or email group with other parents in the classroom where you can check with each other for assistance understanding homework assignments. This is a great tool and enables you to do as much problem solving as possible before contacting the teacher. In this way you can probably complete the work the same day it is assigned, rather than waiting until the following day for teacher contact to occur.

If you are in a dual immersion program, you might think about additional ways to make contacts with other parents in the program for help. One teacher notes, "I am in a two-way immersion program, so I would encourage parents to connect with a family who speaks a different home language to get support." Helping each other to make the most of the language immersion life is just good sense and helps you form wonderful supportive relationships with other families.

> *"Have your child hook up with a homework buddy of the opposite language." – Kathleen J, Language Immersion Educator*

If you have used a variety of strategies to work through understanding an assignment with your child, and have tried working with other parents as well, do let the teacher know the difficulties you continue to have. This will help the teacher make adjustments on future assignments to clarify instructions for you. Also, you may be able to work with the teacher to come up with a plan that works for all concerned to better enable your child to make the home-school connection. Your child will then know that both you and the teacher will continue to expect accountability for homework completion. Knowing that you are united helps children know the boundaries and expectations you share. This will help bring homework battles to an end. Of course, if your child is extraordinarily creative, you and the teacher will have to keep upping your game to stay ahead of new methods for avoiding homework.

Conquer Organization

At times, lack of organization seems to be a student's barrier to success. If you have reason to believe there might be homework, but your child never seems to bring it home, first check with the teacher or the teacher's website to see if this is the expectation. Most teachers are great communicators and contact continues to improve with all the digital tools available to teachers and families.

Often the problem lies in "backpack" issues. Imagine that you are settled in at home in the evening with dinner bubbling on the stove. Everyone is tired, but relaxed. You check the website and see that your child is to complete a task started at school that day. When you ask your child to see the paper from her backpack, you find out that of course, it's not there, but in her desk or locker at school, which is now locked. Three possibilities occur to you: (1) your child intentionally "forgot" the work at school; (2) your child truly doesn't know what happened to it; or (3) your child now remembers that she left it at school.

Any of these three scenarios, if happening consistently, requires a plan of action. The sooner your child develops homework accountability—particularly in a language immersion program where communication requires an extra layer of processing—the better for the stress levels of all involved. It is important to first develop a plan with your child, possibly a positive-reinforcement reward system, to increase consistency in bringing home school assignments. If this doesn't work, once again, contact the teacher.

The organization hurdle affects the path in both directions, to and from school. Students also spend time completing work at home and then "forget" to take it back to school. Why? This is a puzzle that parents, teachers and administrators have worked on for years. Each child presents a new adventure in discovering motives for behavior. Your child's teachers are likely to have many tricks up their sleeves for working with you and your child to increase the homework behaviors you all want to see. No two teachers, two grades, or two schools will approach this the same way. Again, talk with teachers often to clarify the strategies and techniques that work for the teacher, your child, and your family. Keep that teamwork going!

Prioritize Reading Time

The request that you read with your child will most likely be heard from any elementary teacher whether in immersion or in a school where English is the language of instruction. In an immersion school, however, this activity is critical. By reading in English at home on a regular basis you are preparing your child for second grade when English will be introduced. You are increasing your child's English vocabulary and understanding of literary sentence structure and dialogue every time you open a book. If you point at the words as you read, your child learns that those symbols on the page represent the words you are speaking. They intuitively learn that reading goes from left to right, and that the page on the left is read before the page on the right in English. You are teaching reading skills just by sharing this special activity and time with your child.

> *"Read to your child in English if English is his/her first language. If English is his/her second language continue to model your first language at home. Time spent with first language is NOT wasted and will pay off long term in second language acquisition."*
> *– Kathleen J, Language Immersion Educator*

In second grade, when instruction in English reading usually starts, your child's transition from target language reading to English reading will happen quickly, often overnight. You will have given them the vocabulary they need. Remember that your child is already fluent in English. This is their native language. At school they learn to read in the target language, but that does not supplant the native language. Spending time reading together, talking together, and playing together will help the transition from the target language to English go seamlessly.

Macartney (2011), includes these ideas in her list for homework success:

- *Allow your child to explain the concept in English. Then, support the transfer to the target language.*
- *Use English to compare, not to translate. Identify words in the target language that look or sound similar to English. Discuss meanings, pronunciation and structure.*
- *Use a dictionary, thesaurus and other books to demonstrate age-appropriate research skills.*
- *Read, read, read. Read together.*
- *Tell stories and encourage your child to tell stories too. The better your child can tell a good story, the better they will be able to write a good story. Have them add description and sensory details.*
- *Show them you value both English and the target language.*

Many parents say, "My child already knows how to read in English!" In this case, follow your child's natural rhythm and flow. Sometimes they will want to read in English and other times in their school language. In the early years you just need to insist on reading. If your child can read already, take turns each reading a page. Let your child lead. Don't force the issue. Just enjoy the reading time together and make it as consistent as tooth brushing. Keep it up even after your child becomes a competent reader. There is still benefit from reading together, even in the upper grades, if only for the time of close connection and for reinforcing the importance of reading as a valued lifetime skill.

> *"My parents would always let me read to them and talk to them in Spanish, even though they didn't speak Spanish despite their best efforts at trying to learn while I was in kindergarten." – Cecelia R, Former Language Immersion Student*

"My parents tried their best and made sure I still did my homework."
– Former Language Immersion Student

Gain Perspective

Indeed, homework and school projects present one of the major worries of parents in immersion education. Many surveyed parents either listed this as one of their fears or one of their struggles as they went through the program.

"I was worried that I wouldn't be able to help with homework if needed." – Kim T, Language Immersion Parent

"What scared me was not being able to help with homework and not understanding what the teacher was telling my child." – Mindy P, Language Immersion Parent

One day however, parents will have the perspective from the other end of the K-12 experience and realize that what seems like a huge mountain today is really a small molehill. During that time, though, when it appears to be a mountain, it is normal for some kids to take the straight route directly to the top of the homework mountain while others sort of meander around awhile, following the switchbacks on the trail. Whether direct, or meandering, the path gets students to the same place. Now that I've used that example, I need to reiterate that it really is more like a molehill. It's all in your perspective.

I often told parents who were upset about a single homework assignment, "Really, it's a blip on the screen. It's a blip in the context of this particular unit (chapter, or topic), it's a blip in the context of this third grade year, and it's most certainly a blip on their entire life." Just as a "blip" is a small spot of light on a display screen, a piece of homework is a small spot in your child's entire education. Get through it. Move on. All will be well.

Finally, remember to relax and approach this part of the language immersion life with good parenting skills. When asked for their best advice to parents regarding homework, teachers respond repeatedly, "Relax!" and "Stay positive!" No other comments come up more. Love your child, provide emotional support and continue to enrich the student's life at home in as many ways as possible. Exude confidence in your child. Most students remember their parents as being "highly confident about my success in language immersion." Very few recall their parents having any concerns at all. They believed their parents mostly were very confident that everything would work out, and that helped them become more confident.

> *"My parents believed that immersion education was a positive challenge for me. They supported me in school and were confident that I would have success. If they had concerns, they never expressed these to me."* –Allison M, Former Language Immersion Student

> *"Honestly, it was easy. We couldn't help the kids a lot with their homework, but we just trusted that it was going well."* – Julie C, Language Immersion Parent

> *"It will be OK. Most of the time parents are far more stressed out about immersion than the kids. To the kids, it's normal and fun."* – Patrick S, Language Immersion Teacher

Your child is going to the immersion school for their academic and language learning. From you they get a full childhood and happy family life in whatever form that takes. Get through the homework hurdle as early as possible, establish good habits, and sit back and enjoy the effort you put in as your child enters those pre-adolescent and teenage years. Your future self will thank you. Eventually, someday far, far in the future, maybe your child will thank you too!

CHAPTER 7
Active Involvement in Your Child's Experience

I like to think of this learning experience as the "Language Immersion Life" rather than language immersion school or language immersion education. When you choose language immersion for your child, you adopt a lifestyle that comes as part of the package—you become an immersion family. The experience is not drastically different from what it would be in an English-only school, but there are added dimensions that definitely change the direction of your family life.

Language Immersion parents tend to be highly engaged in the school, in after-school programs, and in every aspect of their children's academic and social life. Immersion parents take extra steps to research and then enroll their child in the program, and most likely go through a lottery to secure a spot in the kindergarten class. They also know that they will have more challenges and are willing to invest the time and effort to overcome them because they value the end result—bilingualism and expanded opportunities. By their very nature, they are proactive individuals who do not leave their child's education to chance.

> "Immersion parents are a special breed. We're more involved in our kids' educations, more intense and, truth be told, a little more controlling than most parents. Please remember that you cannot make your school perfect. You can do your best to make it better, and supplement at home what it can't do. Know that your child will be fine either way—kids (are) a lot more resilient than we give them credit for." (Weise 2014)

The school both benefits and suffers from the extra involvement of immersion parents. As Weise indicates, at times parents can be more controlling, but, as an immersion school principal, I was grateful for the tremendous support the school received from parents in terms of time and energy. Quite frankly, schools receive substantial benefits due to the involvement of parents. The daily lives of both teachers and students are enriched through this generous engagement, assistance, and fresh flow of energy and ideas.

> *"I felt like I was surrounded by kids that had very involved parents. There was a higher educational expectation we all shared."*
> *– Former Language Immersion Student*

If you are involved in the early years of the development of a language program you will be heavily involved in its success. The schools I worked with each had a first class of students, called the "pioneer" class. Even though the students were the pioneer students, it was really the parents who were the true pioneers. They were the ones who took a chance on the unknown. They were there every day, helping those of us developing the program and assisting however they could.

> *"He was in the 'pioneer class.' Our concerns resulted from not knowing what was next. Would there be buses? Would there be a*

4th, 5th, 6th grade? Would there be books, an art teacher, a music program? Would he fall behind?" – Catherine C-H, Language Immersion Parent

"Being the first immersion class, everything was being developed as we went along. First there were transportation issues, then teachers, books, and curriculum. Everything was new and constantly changing." – Language Immersion Parent

"It would have been great to have the resources that the immersion students have now. We didn't have very many books. Our teachers did amazing work with the little they had." – Talley S, Former Language Immersion Student

The pioneer class of parents needed even greater trust that this would be a successful program because so much was unknown. Decisions were constantly being made as concerns arose, materials were not always in place, staffing was often completed quite late, transportation offerings were often unclear, and many more unknowns faced these pioneers. I found that because of this uncertainty they were willing to put in even greater effort to ensure we had what we needed on a regular basis. If your family is entering an established program, be thankful that the pioneer parents were willing to pave the way and make your experience smoother, following a somewhat clearer path. If you are a pioneer parent, be ready for uncertainty and prepare yourself to enjoy the experience and its challenges.

Family Life as Support for your Child

Language immersion graduates have noted repeatedly the impact of their parents' support as they went through the program.

> *"Having parental support made a great difference. Sometimes you felt on your own because not all parents speak Spanish. My parents tried their best to understand, and I think they put extra effort into helping me with tough studies."* — Former Language Immersion Student

> *"They sought out ways to get involved even though they spoke NO Spanish. They found their own way to show us how our education was beneficial."* – Talley S, Former Language Immersion Student

When surveyed, the most common item noted by graduates (92%) regarding their parents' support was "just being there and being involved," while 59% noted "encouraging me when I was frustrated" as a common feature of support. Only 38% of students commented on their parents "helping with homework," though it was the biggest concern voiced by parents. There are many ways to support your child and make the immersion experience seem as natural as going to any elementary school. You will discover that support for your child's adventure in the language immersion life extends beyond the schoolhouse door.

An immersion program in Hawaii, at the Papahana Kaiapuni school, noted parent activities leading to student success included providing books, dictionaries and computer programs in both Hawaiian and English for their children to read at home; having frequent contact with teachers through calls, written communications, open houses, conferences, PTA meetings and informal chats when dropping or picking up their children; attending school functions; fundraising and volunteering; assisting both in the classroom and with curriculum preparation tasks outside the classroom; checking for homework completion and reading with children at home; serving on curriculum committees and being politically active to advocate for their school. These immersion parents noted that their involvement affected their children by developing positive values, promoting family bonding, helping with their children's English language learning, and helping the entire family learn about the target language and culture. Volunteer work also seemed to help create a sense of community in the program as families worked together and got to know each other better (Yamauchi, Lau-Smith and Luning 2008).

Global topics tend to come up often in immersion schools, and you will want to support your child's burgeoning interest in the world as a whole. You can be involved by scanning for global programming on TV and the Internet; visiting your local library to see what resources are available for further capitalizing on new interests your child may exhibit; and also by following local opportunities for cultural festivals, restaurants, museum exhibitions and community events. All of these will involve you as parents and will also serve as a means to draw in any siblings who might be attending other schools or programs. These activities also serve to reinforce in English the content your child is learning in the target language. This can help alleviate concerns you may have about lack of English instruction and also helps solidify connections in your child's brain for new learning.

When my older son entered first grade in the immersion program, he developed a robust interest in both Russia and Japan. For an enrichment activity, his teacher encouraged him to research information and write a book about each of these topics. This was followed by projects on New Zealand and Zimbabwe. You will find that immersion teachers tend to be interested in cultures all over the world. Through classroom discussions or their reading selections, they will pass these interests on to their students. As a family we helped our son study these topics, ensuring he had the materials needed. He then wrote illustrated books in Spanish to share with the class and his enthusiastic and encouraging teacher.

Teachers' personal interests may also include certain animals, plants or any number of other world concepts. These interests are quite often transmitted to their students, a phenomenon that occurs in traditional schools as well. However, due to the time invested in cross-cultural settings by immersion teachers, they tend to bring global interests into the classroom more frequently. Immersion students are interested in zebras because they are interested in Africa. They are interested in Africa because they are learning the song "África" in Spanish in music class, or their teacher has been to Africa, has family from or in Africa, or is concerned about health and social issues in Africa.

These interests all may be passed on to students either directly or indirectly. The same can be said for pandas in China, Celtic art and leprechauns in Ireland, trolls in Norway or Farsi in Iran, all subjects my own children wanted to learn about because of the global nature of their teachers. Of course, this doesn't even begin to touch on the cultural connections and backgrounds teachers have with target language communities. These connections are constant in the classroom and shared in great abundance. When your child demonstrates enthusiasm about a new topic, be sure to provide lots of support in developing those interests further. Ask questions about the topic, and let your child be the instructor in passing those cultural tidbits on to you.

> *"I believe the greatest impact was the cultural and global awareness. Their friends came from many different backgrounds and ethnicities. Having teachers from different countries who shared their experiences with the students was amazing. I found that the teachers were all so approachable and ready to share with parent volunteers as well as students. It was a very family involved experience!" – Deb H, Language Immersion Parent*

Other Fun Family Support Activities

There are many ideas for supporting your child at home and you will continue to think of more as your child grows. Some ideas other parents have generated are:

a) If you have multiple children in the immersion program, have a target language dinner or other designated time when siblings can speak the language with each other. You could play "beat the clock" to see if you can lengthen the time they sustain language use until you get it up to at least half an hour. You could create a reward system toward a special family activity together when they have completed a goal number of hours speaking the target language.

b) Seek out a pen pal in another country and provide supplies and motivation to begin a correspondence with this target language friend.

c) Have sleepovers with friends from school. You may just be lucky enough to overhear them speaking to each other, singing, or even arguing in the target language. This is all good stuff! Award special prizes for extended periods of time spent in the target language rather than English.

d) Take your family to markets, festivals, museums, and restaurants that are connected to the target language and culture—anywhere to increase the odds that your child will have an opportunity to speak or even just hear the language in an authentic setting other than school.

e) Travel if you have the time and resources. If you really want to hear your child speak the target language, travel to a place where it is spoken, whether another country or another neighborhood. Language immersion teachers have heard numerous stories about their students' travels and experiences interpreting for their families. These activities occur in a natural setting, so your child is more likely to engage freely in the language experience.

"When we were traveling in Costa Rica, we stayed at a resort for locals rather than international travelers. In the pool one day, they spoke with other kids and taught them how to play Marco Polo, a game none of them had heard of. I told my kids to imagine the local kids going home and teaching their friends to play—they could have started something in motion because of their language skills. Now imagine if they used those skills to convey something other than a game." – Lisa M, Language Immersion Parent

f) If your local high school has foreign exchange students, offer to host one in your home. This not only helps the exchange student, but also provides a wonderful and natural experience for your child to have additional time speaking the language they are learning at school. If you can't commit to hosting, offer to have these students over for dinner or include them in a family activity. This gives the host family a little break and provides your family with an enriching experience.

g) If your school has teaching assistants from other countries, consider offering the same hosting and social activities listed above for foreign exchange students. Anyone who is far from home is often lonely, has few resources, and appreciates any experiences you can offer. Invite them when you go sledding, apple picking, or to any number of family events. Your children will enjoy this as much as the invited guest most certainly will. The Robbinsdale Spanish Immersion School has a robust program with a long history of hosting teaching assistants from Spanish-speaking countries, a program mostly funded by parent fundraising. Many surveyed students fondly recall these assistants living in their home for a semester or a year. Both students and parents liked the built-in resource for homework advice as well as the enrichment provided to their family. Lifelong friendships have been formed, and many hosts visit their former assistants' families back in their home country as well.

h) Try to find babysitters who speak the target language.

i) When there are special projects due at school, invite friends over to work on them together. When talking about schoolwork, children often slip into their target language unintentionally. Increasing opportunities for language use is a goal you should constantly seek to expand. I have many memories of my sons and their friends working on schoolwork with friends at our dining room table, followed by "fun" time. It was incredible listening to them switch back and forth between their two languages in a non-school setting.

j) Have your child/family volunteer at an organization where most people speak the target language. Students report experiences working at food banks, volunteering at clinics, helping with holiday goodwill projects, and many others—all providing time with native speakers.

k) Investigate the wealth of computer programs, apps and websites that utilize the target language. Check the TV schedule to identify target language programs that might be available. Sporting events are sometimes broadcast in the target language and older students in particular enjoy being able to understand the commentators. Younger children enjoy animated programs that utilize the target language. Seek out any and all language input that your family can watch or participate in together through television and technology. It is a benefit for your child to see you engage in these activities as well. Increasing time immersed in cultural and language experiences through these electronic venues expands the immersion experience beyond the school day for your child. It also provides bonding time for you as a family, providing you are doing it together.

Parent Organizations

Important for any elementary school parent, but especially so in a language immersion program, the school-based parent organization is a really critical connection for your family. The parent organization not only is the conduit for providing a great deal of assistance in the school, but also becomes a support group and quite possibly even a pseudo-therapy group for parents. You find that you are all working together to understand this method of learning for your child. You also encounter parents with older children who have already gone through what you are experiencing and have a wealth of information about negotiating this path. You will gain some wonderful friends who have similar values and interests simply because they too have chosen this life for their children.

An active parent organization can really make the difference in the success of an immersion school. There is never enough money in the budget to supply all the needs of any classroom, let alone when that classroom needs to be stocked with materials in two languages. Fundraising to help provide technology and materials for classrooms and libraries is a crucial part of the parent organization. Immersion programs often use cultural celebrations and family-type activities as opportunities to raise funds, while also bringing the school community together for socialization.

Each school I have been involved with has held a large cultural event each year: a fiesta, a carnival or festival. These events require a huge number of volunteers, and parents are the key component that makes these events possible. Students look forward to the event each year. One example is the *Fiesta Fun Fair* of the Robbinsdale Spanish Immersion program. This is an enormous event that generates genuine excitement in students. The school carnival also presents an opportunity for parents to have fun with their children in a cultural setting. Parents can spend time socializing with each other and program staff as their children engage in games and contests. This festival is usually the single largest fundraiser the school will hold. It frequently helps support other student events as well as provide curricular and classroom materials. This part of your child's education is critical. Be involved. Go to these school fundraising events. Let your child learn about community service by first seeing you involved in helping out at school carnivals, pancake breakfasts, movie nights and cultural celebrations. This is often the first place children learn how a community thrives through the participation of its citizenry.

If your school already has an active parent group, get involved at the committee level if you can. Don't think you are too busy. Everyone is busy. Make this a priority for the first five or six years of your child's schooling. Decide you will commit to a certain number of hours per month and then do it. Don't think they already have all the help they need. Offer, offer and offer again.

Fathers, please don't think that this is a "mom's" organization. It may have that appearance, but I guarantee there are tasks that need your special skills and your child needs to see parents of both genders engaged in the school. My husband served on the PTO board when our children were in school. As a school administrator, I have been fortunate to have the assistance of many fathers at school events over the years. At the Ada Vista Spanish Immersion school, the fathers held a pancake breakfast, completely a "fathers' gig." Though not a dad, as the school principal I was allowed access, to observe their camaraderie and engagement in the work for their children. As a teacher, I watched time and again the pride of students when their fathers would serve as chaperones on school field trips. You are a language immersion family, and this is only enhanced by the involvement of all family members.

Classroom Assistance

Another way to improve your child's experience in elementary school is through your involvement at the classroom level. All elementary teachers need help and support in the classroom due to the time-consuming nature of planning. This is even truer when the teacher is preparing lessons in a second language, or after first grade, in two languages. Classroom materials in the target language, while becoming more plentiful each year, are still not as prolific as in English. Teachers either have to conduct lengthy searches, or create curriculum materials themselves. Support from parents is infinitely valuable. It frees up precious planning time that teachers can then dedicate to curricular issues and planning valuable experiences for your child.

You can be a great support by volunteering on a regular basis in your child's classroom. You will need to approach the teacher to ask how you can be of assistance. Offer early in the year, but be aware that the teacher may not be ready at that time because they are still setting up routines and getting to know their students. Continue to offer on a regular basis throughout the year. Sometimes parents complain, "I offered, but was never called." This happens because teachers have so many details and decisions facing them each day that sometimes it's hard to identify immediately how parents can be of help. Continue offering, and a path will emerge at some point during the year. In my own classroom I often asked parents to complete a survey at the beginning of the year. I would suggest skills I was looking for and ask parents to suggest additional ways they could help. Your child's teacher may have a similar system. Common practices include sign-up charts outside the classroom door, sign-ups at parent night, website volunteer check boxes, or other means for letting the teacher know of your interests. Other teachers prefer to request help as needed. School policies vary with regard to how much time parents are allowed in classrooms and in the school building and for what purposes. Learn about the policies and assist within that framework.

Sometimes it doesn't occur to teachers that parents truly are willing to do some of the detail work for them. So if you see something in the classroom that you could have done, offer your assistance, again highlighting that particular activity. "I would have been willing to assemble those folders for you. Please feel free to call me to drop in and help out." This may help a teacher realize the kinds of things you are willing to do. For example, I had parents come in an hour each week to run photocopies, water the plants in my classroom, change bulletin boards, display student art in the halls, and assemble folders for conferences. Some of these things take small amounts of time, when you might be at the school anyway, but manage to cross one thing off the teacher's to-do list.

Offer services for things you can do at home as well. Don't be offended, however, if your PhD in history, your MBA, or nursing degree is underutilized to cut out flower shapes or staple book pages together. These are necessary tasks that make your child's school day more enjoyable, but often get shoved aside by the important academic preparation activities the teacher needs to pursue. Be willing to do the mundane tasks, so your child's teacher can use their skills to focus on your child's education. These simple projects can be done at home while sitting with your child at the homework table, while watching a football game, or sitting and waiting at a child's extracurricular activities. I once took valentine heart patterns to cut out at my son's basketball game. I learned that day to pack a few extra pencils and scissors in my bag, because other parents were offering to help as well!

Not every immersion teacher welcomes parents spending time in the classroom. The parent's English-language influence interferes with the cultural island the teacher is trying to create. This is a valid concern of teachers. Immersion staffs work diligently to keep all input in the target language, and then, in a matter of minutes, a parent volunteer can unwittingly sabotage this effort by speaking in English to students in the classroom. Even in school hallways, spoken English serves as a distraction to children. Accept this and really try to honor the efforts that the language immersion staff is making to enhance the immersion setting for all children. Try not to speak in English at all or speak in a soft voice so it is not easily overheard.

> *"Spanish-speaking parents are welcome to help in my classroom during learning stations. That means they can work with a small group to reinforce concepts already taught. English-speaking parents are welcome to volunteer to work in the classroom but not with students. We try to protect and treasure our Spanish time, so bringing English in at the wrong time causes students to lose valuable language-learning time that they need. As students are beginning to think and function in Spanish, the last thing they need is some English thrown in there to switch their brains back into English and make them have to start over again to get back into the Spanish-language flow." – Rebecca G, Language Immersion Educator*

> *"Parents want to be involved in their kids' education and that involvement is good for kids. They need to understand why they need to refrain from speaking English while we are in Spanish time, but beyond that, I think the involvement of parents should be welcomed." – Laura M, Language Immersion Teacher and Parent*

Make an attempt to see how you can volunteer in other ways in the school or classroom. Many teachers will offer you options, such as materials preparation, classroom décor, center setup, photocopying, and a multitude of other tasks that are necessary for the smooth operation of a classroom. If left to the teacher, these duties would take away from time better spent preparing lessons or reviewing student work. Often, in this scenario, a parent will report to the classroom, pick up a project from the teacher, and go to another part of the school, such as the library or even a hallway, to complete the work.

> *"Be willing to volunteer in areas other than in the classroom. We need lots of help in other areas as well: library, cafeteria, recess, organizing/preparing for projects, etc."* – Kristi H, Language Immersion Educator

> *"I LOVE my parent volunteers."* – Jane P, Language Immersion Teacher

Some teachers, however, will welcome your presence most any time in the classroom and give you organizational activities to complete within the room. These might include sorting and preparing materials, updating bulletin boards, organizing art materials, or any of the numerous tasks that go into making elementary school a delightful experience. Other teachers may have you work with small groups of children or one-on-one with students on skills that are taught in English. If you also possess the target language skills, you may be asked to assist with reading, math or editing writing projects. Be prepared to assist in the way the teacher most needs help. It is difficult for a teacher when parents would like to volunteer but only want to do a particular type of activities. Be flexible in your support, and you will continue to be offered opportunities to contribute.

If you assist inside the classroom when students are present, remember to avoid using English as much as possible. Children will approach you and try to engage you in English. Use hand signals to show that you aren't going to talk right now and just assist without speaking. Always follow the directions of the teacher in this regard, as each has individual preferences. Your volunteer work is to *help* the teacher, not create a distraction for the teacher and the students in the room.

> *"Parents need to know that they are welcome to volunteer but it is extremely important to not speak in English in the classroom.*

> *The entire school is fostering the second language in announcements, symbols, signs and communication. Teachers speak Spanish between themselves and try not to utter words in English. Parents need to understand and honor that. Ask the school how you can help support them in their efforts. Trust them."* – Amie S, Language Immersion Educator

Your own child can cause one of the biggest distractions while you are volunteering. Your child will have a difficult time distinguishing between your role as classroom volunteer and your role as parent. When you enter the room, your child will expect you to act as the parent and to treat them differently than the other children. Have a talk with your child prior to volunteering to help them understand that you are not "Mommy" or "Daddy" in the classroom. Rather, you are a teacher assistant and your child is just another student in the classroom. Make sure your child understands this distinction and insist that they abide by it. I find this is harder for parents than for children, so toughen up and treat your child the same as any other student in the classroom while volunteering. A quick smile, wink or wave to recognize your special relationship when you enter the room is the goal you are working for. Extended hugging, kissing, and talking are distracting to all students and the teacher as well. Save those activities for times when you are not "on duty" as a parent volunteer. Also, try as hard as possible to leave younger siblings at home or with a babysitter, as their presence is very distracting for all students, the teacher, and you as well.

There are so many ways to volunteer both in the classroom and in the school as a wider entity. Schools benefit from help in nearly every area. I can't imagine ever getting the doors of our school open without the many parents who came to help out in the office, gardening in front of the school, unpacking the countless boxes of materials, hanging flags, and making signs. Whatever strength you have to offer, do it! Or try something new that isn't your strength.

You just might be surprised by newfound skills. Plus, you are modeling risk-taking for your child.

Family Networking

As a school administrator, it has been fun to follow families that have grown into lifelong friends due to the close bonding that occurs as their children grow together in the immersion program. Through your children, you will begin a long alliance of family support and assistance. This networking starts at the school, but continues as children start visiting each other's homes for play dates and birthday parties. Participation in sports teams, clubs, dance, music, and other activities also draws immersion families together. Language immersion children usually gain friends from other schools at these events, but have a strong tendency to socialize with each other due to their common backgrounds. It naturally follows that parents begin relationships through carpools, sitting in bleachers, and taking turns hosting the kids. These alliances then grow into true friendships that become the best support system for life as immersion families.

I am aware of more than one group of parents who became friends when their children were in kindergarten and still get together socially, even though their children have graduated from college. In Minnesota, a group of immersion parents still gets together to watch their sons play softball each summer. Those sons are now in their mid-thirties! Growing up together as children and aging together as adults forms the basis for really strong friendships between families living the language immersion life.

> *"The greatest impact has been the quality of the peer group among the immersion kids and their families. This group has been those active volunteers who continuously showed up to get things done for the school." – Language Immersion Parent*

> *"I am so beyond thankful for my times in language immersion. Not only were they some of the most memorable times in my life, but I also think they impacted my education greatly. I made lasting friendships that have gotten me through all of high school and college.... I would do it all over again in a heartbeat."*
> – *Former Language Immersion Student*

> *"I have still kept in touch with many of my immersion friends – the uniqueness of our experience has bonded us like siblings."*
> – *Anita M, Former Language Immersion Student*

> *"I have hated and loved this program, it gets hard and sometimes you get to the point where you want to quit. But if you think about it in the long run it will take you very far and you create these long-lasting friendships with other immersion kids that you can't get anywhere else. We're all a family and we have been from the start."*
> – *Skylar S, Former Language Immersion Student*

Parent Involvement in the Secondary Immersion Program

Your role as parent definitely changes as your child enters the middle or junior high school years and even more so in the high school years. Of course this role change is true for any parent of a teenager, whether in immersion education or not. Your child most likely will not want to see you at school so often. However, due to the tight bonds formed by families in the elementary years, secondary immersion students tend to be less resistant to family involvement than many other students of this age.

Even so, this is a time of greater independence for your child, so your role will definitely change to more of a program advocate rather than classroom volunteer. Johnson (2003) has identified several ways parents can help in secondary immersion programs:

- Organize meetings to bring the immersion group (parents, staff, students) together for social activities.
- Advocate with district officials to ensure continuing program support.
- Make sure your administrators are aware of your passion about immersion.
- Offer to assist in providing information administrators may need.
- Create a listserv, Facebook group, or other mailing list for parents to continue networking.
- Ensure immersion is represented on building and district committees.
- Help to organize field trips and travel opportunities.
- Organize a unified parent group to work with the district or school.

I'm sure parents will be able to identify other ways to volunteer that are specific to your own school setting, but this list provides a great start to ways you can stay involved. Your children will still recognize your involvement and participation in their educational experience without being obtrusive in their own teenage adventure. In addition, you are providing a support to those secondary teachers that they don't usually receive from parents. The concepts of the volunteering you did in the elementary years continue to apply, teachers at this level still can use assistance with mundane tasks so that they can focus on the education of your child.

> *"Parents need to stay engaged at the secondary level. Because the entire focus of the middle or high school is not immersion, these*

> *programs can start to feel a little forgotten. Parents that can stay involved need to help immersion teachers with planning events, trips, speakers, and extension activities that can help promote the program and make it more visible to the rest of the community. For example, create a niche for students—have a logo, t-shirts, water bottles, posters. Make it look like a community within the school. Parents can take this on because teachers are busy with academics and administrators are focused on other issues. Parents can help. Kids totally love t-shirts."* – Erik M, Language Immersion Educator and Former Student

Parent groups have great power to influence opportunities for their children in the immersion program. Be sure not to let the excitement, passion and involvement of the elementary grades die down once your child becomes more independent at the secondary level. Often this is the most important time for parents to unify and let their voices be heard. Continued involvement will help maintain the continuity and strength of the language immersion program both during the years your child attends, and for the years that follow.

CHAPTER 8
The Secondary School Experience: Long-Term Commitment

"At every new school we went to we were the freaks . . . The transition between programs was big in many ways. We moved schools and met new teachers and peers . . . it always seemed as though it took a little extra time to get into the groove of things . . . Hard as it was to be the freaks and constantly be underestimated by our teachers I feel so lucky to have been in language immersion. It's been quite fun to be a pleasant surprise to my university professors."
– Maria B, Language Immersion Student (Blonigan 2001)

Most parents who choose language immersion are principally concerned about elementary education and offering their children the opportunity to take advantage of the early language acquisition that occurs so easily for them. It is only when their child arrives in the upper elementary grades that the idea of middle and high school learning starts to take center stage. Now what?

Sadly, many school districts don't start planning early enough for the development of this "now what" stage for immersion students. If you are considering a program with a long history, the district has most likely addressed many of the struggles in providing for the continued education of immersion students. If you are in a newer program, be prepared to fight for the needs of your children as they go through secondary school. Families commonly experience frustration in the early years of a program's development. Most wish the path had been laid out for them more fully. They often are surprised to learn that the secondary program hasn't been developing along with the elementary program but that, instead, they are at square one again, just as they were when their child started kindergarten. Immersion parents who were surveyed in different states expressed the exact same frustrations about secondary immersion education.

"We're grateful for the continuation of the immersion experience in middle school because that was essential for language maintenance. Sometimes I wonder about the district's choice of which subject areas to teach in Spanish." – Jennifer H, Language Immersion Parent

"I felt early on that there was very little guidance to parents or student about what options were available. If you didn't have a friend in the upper class to guide you through the process, you're really blind. Administrators have done a much better job in recent years informing the parents of the various choices available." – Krista F, Language Immersion Parent

"Lot of tweaks and program changes but for me it's all to be expected. Middle school was the hardest because issues on Spanish grammar were just being identified. Passionate parent mentality reared it's ugly head again, not trusting the system." – Karen C, Language Immersion Parent

"The 'path' issue was big for everyone but it seems everyone is recognizing the journey is as unique as the student. A little more guidance and leadership versus 'figure it out class by class' would help." – Language Immersion Parent

"The 'roadmap' for middle and high school was weak. We seemed to be building the airplane in the air." – Language Immersion Parent

Immersion programs tend to be developed by enthusiastic elementary educators and then students are passed on to secondary programs. Teachers and administrators in the secondary programs often do not have the opportunity to provide input until a very late stage—if at all. In addition, language immersion often is only part of a secondary teachers assignment. They are dividing their time between their other secondary students and the immersion students. It is not their complete focus. This is true as well for administrators who have multiple programs in their buildings to supervise. In the elementary experience, administrators and teachers often only have immersion students and they are more focused on immersion goals within their program.

The division of course and program assignments, and therefore divided focus at the secondary level, may explain why secondary staff members frequently do not receive the training and time to prepare and understand immersion education. However, parents still expect the same high quality program they received in elementary school. On the other hand, elementary teachers are not given the opportunity and time to provide guidance and direction to the secondary program. Thus, frustration ensues for everyone. A teamwork approach between elementary and secondary administrators, teachers and parents is important and should guide the entire immersion experience. It is wise to recognize early on as you enter the secondary years that immersion is but one part of that experience from both the school's perspective and most likely, your child's as well.

"Programs after the elementary years can lose their identity. It becomes 'classes that are offered' instead of a program that is an

integral facet of the educational experience. The cohesiveness and mentality of it being a 'program' can be lost. It is important for parents to continue to support the program and actively work toward the 'program' continuing through the secondary years." – Erik M, *Language Immersion Educator and Former Student*

There are numerous successful K-12 immersion programs throughout the country upon which a district may model its own program development. However, early in the development of immersion programs, school administrators and boards of education generally are not truly aware of what commitment they are making to immersion families, and are not prepared for the specialized education immersion students need. In addition, many secondary teachers are not prepared for immersion students and their unique needs. They are generally supportive of having these students in their classes, but then are surprised by the differences in their skills compared to other students. For example, teachers are often dismayed by immersion students' natural flow in speaking and writing, using several connected sentences and paragraphs. These same students, however, show less understanding of grammar rules than their traditional students. Likewise, students in English classes speak and write naturally in English but also sometimes struggle with grammar rules. It's not really a unique or uncommon phenomena but it still comes as a surprise to secondary language teachers.

> *"Rarely were our new teachers confident in our abilities, especially to speak and understand. Often this proved to be our main source of entertainment in the first week of classes....It was only after the first writing assignment that the teacher's disbelief would finally end. Of course, after that we were really in for it. They enjoyed pushing our limits to see how much we actually knew."* –Maria B, *Former Language Immersion Student (Blonigan 2001)*

> "High school was difficult in Spanish because they didn't know what to do with us. We were way beyond any other students they had." – *Catherine E, Former Language Immersion Student*

Many school districts do not adequately offer professional development to their secondary teachers in the understanding and delivery of immersion education. Nor are many secondary teachers given the opportunity to spend time observing the elementary program, so that they are at least aware of what to expect when immersion students enter their classrooms. Often this is due to time, energy, cost of hiring substitute teachers during the observations, or merely because nobody thought of it or realized its importance. As a low cost option for staff development, however, it can be one of the most interesting, revealing and effective uses of professional time. Secondary teachers can learn quickly and precisely what goes on in immersion classrooms and what language skills students will have when entering the secondary arena, much in the same way your visits to the immersion school enlighten you on how the program works.

The Entering Secondary Immersion Student

> "How was it? Great! It was actually nice going through middle and high school with my immersion family." – *Katie Jo J-B, Language Immersion Student*

Graduates of elementary immersion programs generally demonstrate remarkable skill in listening, reading, writing and speaking in the target language. This does not mean there are no language errors when they exercise these skills. Elementary students learn from modeling, not grammar instruction. Therefore language refinement needs to occur at the secondary level. In elementary school students learn *content* via the target language, not the language specifically as one would in high school or college language classes. They have learned to read and write in the target language with increasing vocabulary and skill in sentence structure, punctuation, and paragraph development, just as they would have in an English-only elementary school. They have not been taught to conjugate verbs, use past and future tenses, parts of speech, and other grammatical features specifically, though they certainly use these skills as they manipulate language.

> *"At the time it was different and I felt as if I was not taught like everyone else in high school who were learning it all. Of course I knew a lot more than others but I didn't even know what the word 'conjugate' meant."* – Former Language Immersion Student

> *"I can use the subjunctive properly in a conversation and in writing, but *#%@*#!! if you make me conjugate that verb on a test."* – John M, Former Language Immersion Student

Immersion students leaving elementary school can speak about life today, yesterday and tomorrow – using the correct verb tense. However, when asked to give the past tense, third-person form of a particular verb, they would be at a loss. They can tell you what they are *doing*, but are clueless about what a present progressive form of a verb might be. These students often make errors, such as dropping direct and indirect objects all over their target language sentences. High school language teachers have a hard time getting their traditional students to use objects at all, let alone *over* use them.

Immersion students hear the target language that includes appropriate uses of grammatical structure from teachers and other speakers all through elementary school. They learn these structures and then sometimes over-apply them in their own language use, using them both correctly in some situations and incorrectly in others. A traditional student most likely will do the opposite, forgetting to include these structures in their language without great amounts of practice. Secondary teachers are often quite surprised that students cannot do many of the grammatical exercises that their regular first-year language students can do. Immersion students, however, have a vast vocabulary for numerous domains and can speak with and understand native speakers with ease. They can also write pages on a topic, albeit with errors, while a first-year language student may struggle to write a single sentence with any depth.

This is where middle and high school language immersion courses come in. A quality secondary program will take the skills of immersion students and refine them, increasing accuracy and building ever-higher levels of what is known as "educated language." The secondary immersion experience is important because it serves as a bridge between the elementary program and the introduction of advanced language courses and preparation for Advanced Placement (AP) and International Baccalaureate (IB) courses and exams.

Immersion students are also on track to take courses at the college level, either through dual enrollment while in high school or later when the student enters post-secondary education. Many students take courses in target-language literature or linguistics at their local colleges after passing the AP exams in high school. Students usually excel in these courses, and receive high praise from college instructors regarding their skills and ability to keep up with college-level language study.

Transition

There tends to be a transition period when students adjust from the full oral language input of the elementary immersion classroom to the new style of the secondary program. Some of the students' classes are taught via language immersion and other classes are taught in English. Immersion students are often mixed with students from English-only programs. It takes time to for immersion students to adapt to working with students from a different educational background as well as teachers with new and different sets of expectations.

> *"The transition from full immersion in the elementary school to partial immersion in middle school and high school was difficult. I think that's the only time my parents worried about me."*
> *–Former Language Immersion Student*

Other students adjust easily, and hardly notice that anything has changed in their educational program. Sometimes they are so busy adjusting to adolescence and all it entails that the changes in their school day don't seem to merit attention.

> *"Middle school transition went extremely well. Socially and emotionally he felt connected to peers from a common immersion experience but also eager to meet the rest of the grade level. He took on the personal responsibility and organization needed for middle level success." – Susan G, Language Immersion Parent and Educator*

Sometimes an immersion student will take a break from immersion for a variety of reasons—a family moves and then returns, an extended illness or injury, or another educational opportunity presents itself that the student pursues. These students often have even greater difficulties transitioning. While I advocate a steady continuance in the program for reasons noted already, I have witnessed a number of students who have left the program and returned to transition successfully. This usually is due to extremely supportive parents and teachers at the middle or high school accepting and working with students to help them reach their goals. As one student writes:

"I took a two-year break from immersion to go to an environmental school, all the while having a tutor in Spanish once a week. The transition back from that school was rough, but smoother than I expected. The immersion teachers were very welcoming and caring. My teachers encouraged me to ask questions so I could understand the things I got wrong. I soon learned how immersion was like one huge family. This helped me grow in so many ways and my future grew in possibilities." – Lydia P, Language Immersion Student

Secondary Options

There are many options for organizing the immersion program at the secondary level, and districts have approached this in different ways. Usually there is not an immersion designated school at the secondary level, but a track within a regular English school in which immersion students can take classes for part of their day. In middle school it is desirable to have about half the day in the target language. Often this is comprised of 2-3 classes, usually including language arts as well as science, health, math or social studies. For example, one model for a middle school offers social studies and science classes in Spanish in 6th grade, and switches to social studies and language arts in 7th grade, followed by "Spanish II Pre-Advanced Placement" in 8th grade (Jones 2005). At the high school level, students sometimes take courses in non-language subject areas that are taught by language teachers. Examples might be social studies or health taught in German by a German teacher. Other times students take courses taught by teachers of the content areas who also happen to be fluent speakers of the target language. For example, a biology teacher who also happens to speak French may offer one section of biology taught in French. In some cases students are given proficiency tests to determine what language course they will take either in an immersion strand or in the regular high school course sequence (Barr-Harrison 2003).

After conducting interviews in seven secondary immersion programs, Montone and Loeb (2003) reported that the most critical factors for determining subjects to be offered in the second language are the availability, qualifications and subject matter preferences of program staff, as well as the availability of appropriate materials in the target language. Sometimes a district cannot or chooses not to staff content classes and folds immersion students into its regular language program. This usually causes difficulties for both immersion and regular students because they possess such different skill sets. Teachers struggle to provide for both sets of students, and find that either the immersion students become bored easily, or their other students are intimidated. No matter which model of elementary immersion a child attended, "no graduate of an elementary school foreign language program should be placed with beginners in the middle or junior high school" (Pesola 1988).

Immersion students often skip the first-year class of a language and test into upper levels. At first they are often frustrated by gaps in their knowledge, but with support they quickly catch up and excel at the upper levels, especially those with great amounts of oral instruction. This is all part of the "polishing and refining" process that needs to occur with immersion students' language. They have a great amount of fluency, but need the refinement of an educated speaker to advance to the next level of skill in the language.

A good secondary program offers a new skill set to the student, the type of language refinement that would occur when a native-speaking child receives an education. This is the time that guiding students toward a more "correct" form of speaking and writing gains steam—while building on the large amount of language acquisition that began in elementary school. This marks the difference between informal and formal means of communication. Students begin to learn more about language proficiency; they can differentiate between times when accuracy is required and when casual communication will permit some errors. Teachers help students learn that communication must be suited to the situation, the people involved, and expectations. Nuances of language are learned at this point, and gentle correction will occur to improve skills, while still maintaining an environment where students feel free to express ideas (Lipton 1998).

The subject content of continued immersion program offerings is not necessarily as important as the additional time studying and learning in the language. Any chosen course content can help students practice and refine their skills. Whether language arts, math, science, social studies, industrial or fine arts, technology, or any other possible course offering—all give students the opportunity to use their language in a communicative setting and increase their vocabulary. A teacher with great language skills can help students by allowing them time to continue reading, writing, listening and speaking. Every school will have different offerings because they have different staff members with varying skills in the target language. Schools also have differing amounts of funding for providing staff to deliver the program. Sometimes schools will seek student and family input in order to match course offerings to their interests. Usually however, decisions regarding course offerings are determined by school staff members available to teach courses to immersion students.

It really doesn't matter what the topic happens to be, the key element is the offering of additional time in the target language for students to continue improving their vocabulary and skill. A study of Canadian French immersion programs looked at content area and determined that language proficiency attained by students taking history and geography courses was no higher than the level reached by students in math and science courses. It was determined that the overall performance in the target language improved in *all* of the content courses studied (Lapkin and Cummins 1984).

Another perk of offering content-based courses is that it enables students to "kill two birds with one stone," or squeeze both a continued language experience and a subject course requirement into one precious time slot in their course schedule. Students have to make many choices, especially if they have other interests such as music or art to pursue. It becomes increasingly difficult for them to maintain their language course sequence, take the large number of graduation requirement and college preparatory courses, and pursue any extra interests. The content-based model, where students take two or three content courses in the immersion language, offers the best opportunity for students to continue their target language, meet graduation requirements, and pursue additional interests.

There are even more variations and models for middle and high school programs than elementary programs. Whichever model is available in your school district, it will provide for some sort of refinement and additional practice in the language. Some schools have mastered the secondary portion better than others but most all programs do the best they can, given cost and time constraints. Generally, the secondary portion of immersion education takes much longer to polish into a smooth, successful program. Many programs struggle and adapt for years before settling on a model that works within their district.

If you are in the early years of a program's development, you should expect to be involved in advocating for the refinement of your program. Elementary programs have greater background, experience and models from which to draw, and are generally started by those who are passionate about immersion education. Secondary programs get immersion graduates handed to them and then must develop a viable program without that early passion that launched the elementary program. Secondary administrators, counselors and teachers cannot be 100% focused on the immersion program as your elementary program might have been. They also have non-immersion students, usually a higher number of them, who require much of their time and attention as well. They simply cannot be dedicated solely to the immersion program. Be understanding that their time is split among *all* the students, staff, and parents in the school and the many needs of everyone. Again, most secondary programs go through several years of trial and error before settling in. In spite of this, most students and parents still feel the immersion experience was worth it—and parents feel it is worth advocating for their children to continue language education in middle and high school. Be patient and be grateful that your child received a great elementary language opportunity and can now progress in whatever way possible.

Secondary Results

Data is scarce about the results of secondary immersion programs. Most of the information available comes from anecdotal evidence of students claiming how easy their high school courses were for them compared with their peers. In college, former immersion students note that they are genuinely surprised by how their skills stack up against those of their peers. This is often when immersion students really start realizing what a gift they have—to be so accomplished in a second language. They also often feel that they are academically superior to their peers in other ways as well.

> *"In addition to learning everything any other child learned in school, I also learned it in a second language. Can't beat that."*
> *– Janet G-M, Former Language Immersion Student*

> *"In my experience in high school the AP and honors classes were always filled with other kids from Spanish immersion, more than non-immersion kids." – Former Language Immersion Student*

> *"I felt I was a bit more cultured than my other friends. I had significantly more knowledge about other cultures." – Shawna V, Former Language Immersion Student*

> *"I came out of the program with a broader cultural appreciation as well as two languages to draw from. That is definitely more than what my peers in English only-programs learned." – Anita M-M, Former Language Immersion Student*

It is notable that 87% of the immersion program graduates responding to my surveys feel they learned a lot more than their friends who were in English-only programs. Either they actually were able to process and learn more through the immersion process, or the experience simply gave them great self-esteem and confidence. Either way, immersion students emerge competent and ready to take on the world.

One program in Texas collected test data on its seventh grade Spanish immersion students by having them take the National Spanish Examination. This test is used to offer high school teachers an evaluation of how the Spanish skills of their students compare nationally with other high school students. Of the 31 seventh graders, 65% were at the 90th percentile, 16% at the 80th percentile, 13% at the 70th percentile and 6% at the 67th percentile. One of their students scored at the 99th percentile! Alamo Heights had much to be proud of with this seventh grade class scoring so high on an exam where they were compared with high school students (Jones 2005). Even without this kind of data, most language immersion educators would credit their students with similar successes, proven by informal evaluation and observation.

> *"Parents always want to compare their child's English progress with their non-immersion neighbor's English progress. This is*

like comparing apples to oranges. Don't do it! It has been proven through research that immersion students will equal or out-perform their non-immersion counterparts. As an immersion middle school teacher for almost a decade, I have seen this with my own eyes. Our students always score well. Once again, relax!" – Amie S, Language Immersion Educator

Additional Language Opportunities

A major impact of immersion education is that students learn to love languages in general. They are interested when they hear others speak a language other than the two they already know, and often want to learn additional languages.

> *"What I love most is that when an individual speaks another language, he tilts his head IN to ask questions and to learn."*
> *– Susan G, Language Immersion Parent and Educator*

In the past I have sometimes heard high school language teachers express concern when an elementary language immersion program is developed in a different language than the one they are teaching. They fear that student numbers will drop in their language classes once those kids reach high school. Often the opposite is true, and they actually gain students from the elementary immersion program who wish to pick up an additional language in high school. In the final years of elementary school teachers often hear their students exclaim that they are ready to take on another language, and soon thereafter, they often do.

Immersion students often add a third language, while continuing study of their first and second languages. The interaction between the language they are beginning to study and the refining of the second language they have been studying for approximately the past seven years presents new challenges and opportunities for those ready for this step. This is yet another benefit of immersion education: by gaining competence in a second language early on, the acquisition of additional languages is far easier.

Spanish immersion student Emily wanted to add French upon reaching high school. She couldn't fit the class into her schedule so ended up taking the class online through a virtual high school. After listening to Emily's French speech recordings, the instructor noted that Emily spoke French much better than many of the instructor's fourth year French students. When Emily stated that she was fluent in Spanish due to having been in an immersion program, the instructor was not surprised, stating that her best students were usually immersion students.

On the other hand, nearly 70% of immersion graduates indicate that they stayed with the elementary school target language and did not take additional languages. Among my survey respondents who did pursue other languages, an additional 17 languages were studied, including European, Slavic, Asian, Mid-Eastern, Ancient, and Sign languages.

> *"I was not able to continue in the immersion program during middle and high school which was a great disappointment. I took French classes and was surprised at the similarities between the two languages. I had significant success in French because of my foundation in Spanish and ranked among the top 5 in the country on national French tests."* – Allison M, Former Language Immersion Student

AP Classes, Placement Exams and Dual Enrollment

Numerous immersion students take Advanced Placement (AP) language classes. A study reported by Lipton, Morgan and Reed, published in volume 21 of the *ATTF National Bulletin* (cited in Lipton 1998) revealed that students who performed best on AP tests were those who indicated they had studied the language in grades 1-3. AP classes prepare students for taking the test by refining their skills and filling in any language gaps that may be left from previous language study. These higher-level classes often consist of immersion students mixed in with those who were enrolled in the traditional high school language program for at least three or more years. Immersion students usually do very well in AP courses, while benefitting greatly from the review of language that occurs.

My older son struggled in his high school level AP prep classes. The grammar, accents and other language details kept him from getting the high grades he was accustomed to, receiving only C's from his language teacher. Every exam came home riddled with red marks noting his grammatical errors. Native speakers had told him since second grade how excellent his Spanish was, so this turn of events was quite difficult for him. When spring came and it was time to take the AP test, his Spanish teacher told him not to take the test because he would certainly fail. As parents, we decided to let him take a gamble on the test, assuming that he could learn from it and re-take it the following year. He ended up getting the highest score possible, something no other student at his high school accomplished that year. Was it his AP class training with the focus on grammar, or the immersion experience of general competence and confidence in the language that helped him get that top score? Most likely, it was a combination of both experiences that helped him with this achievement and enabled him to go on to successful university level language studies.

Other exams that students might take go by many acronyms, such as ACTFL OPI, STAMP, SOPA, and specific tests for each language. Sometimes they are required as part of exiting a high school program, given as part of an award program (such as a National French Exam), or required by some universities when applying. Some schools use these tests as tools for assessing how they are progressing as a program. These are nationally standardized tests for language proficiency and as a rule students have a fair amount of confidence with them.

> *"We automatically get a leg up on formal testing since we are completely used to speaking in long conversations in the target language by the time we take those tests." – Emily P, Former Language Immersion Student*

Immersion students also frequently take placement tests once in college and receive college credit for their high school language courses. Others take college-level dual-enrollment classes at a local college while still in high school. It is important to engage teachers, counselors, and administrators as well as local college staff in order to make these experiences go smoothly.

Of immersion students who later go to college, over 68% receive college credit for their AP exams, placement tests or dual-enrollment. Some report receiving abundant college credits and placing into the highest levels even though they did not take any language classes their final year or two in high school. It's like getting a college scholarship when one receives credit via a free or low-cost method like testing out of coursework. What parent doesn't like reduced tuition bills? Many would concur with the parent whose daughter received a Spanish AP score of 5, earning 16 credit hours at a state university. "This will save us thousands of dollars on tuition. Plus, she is only about two classes away from having a minor in Spanish."

The Long-Term Commitment

Weise (2014) reminds us that "Immersion programs require a long-term commitment" and encourages parents to stick with it until at least eighth grade, citing research that indicates that it takes five to seven years for children to reach a level of academic language skills on par with native speakers. The question of staying with the immersion program is one every family deals with at each level of the educational process. Transition from elementary to secondary has been identified in the long-standing Canadian immersion programs as a time when many students choose not to remain with the immersion model (Boudreaux 2011).

Some students choose not to continue once they leave elementary school and move on to other interests. For example, a student who is musically talented may wish to take multiple music classes and not have room in the schedule for immersion classes. The same may be true for those highly interested in science or any other subject area offered by the school district. Some states have so many course requirements that little choice for each student is allowed. However, if you enlist the assistance of counselors and others at the secondary school level, you may work through many of the hurdles that scheduling may present. Be aware that counselors may not have received any professional development whatsoever about immersion education. They may not understand your commitment to the program, so be prepared to be proactive in making your wishes known.

In addition to scheduling concerns, parental fear presents a principal reason students leave the immersion program at the secondary level. Parents have lost some of their early language learning passion and become concerned about their child having covered all the curricular bases in other subjects. Parents also become concerned about grade point averages, which can have a profound effect on college opportunities.

> Parents who were the ... program's biggest fans when their children were in elementary school can suddenly become less than supportive when the program moves to middle school and especially high school.... [They] may grow more concerned about having their children taught subjects like

math and science in a non-English language, fearing that they will not do as well on standardized tests, such as the SAT, and that participation in the program will ultimately hinder their prospects of gaining entry into a good college or university. (Montone and Loeb 2003)

The fear that staying in the immersion program in high school can hurt a student's GPA and therefore have an effect on opportunities related to college admission and scholarships is understandable. This concern however, usually doesn't come to fruition. Students who stay with immersion education do not suffer from reduced opportunities at the postsecondary level. Numerous students have been accepted into the top universities in the country even though they gave up taking some of their high school offerings in order to continue in their language study. Immersion students simply are not being turned away from universities due to gaps in their education caused by an emphasis on second language coursework. Anecdotal data would indicate that just the opposite is true. Immersion students are valued for their language expertise, as universities are well aware of the need to prepare globally and culturally competent students for the work force.

Immersion educator Boudreaux (2011) suggests that many students leave immersion at the middle school level because the sentiment from the elementary school years when students and families felt very special and closely bonded no longer carries into the middle school. Students are not treated as a unique cohort any longer, but receive instruction with the general population. Many students are ready for this transition and seek out non-immersion friends. Most remain bonded with their immersion peers. However, the general feeling is somehow different and a few students leave immersion once the special nature of their immersion cohort starts to dissipate.

"Middle school can be a trying time for immersion students. Adolescents are very concerned about being different so this is when

many want to leave programs. It is very imperative that parents hold strong and continue to support immersion. I have seen numerous examples of the most resistant middle schoolers becoming the biggest advocates for the immersion experience." – Patrick S, Language Immersion Educator

Another reason for leaving the immersion model is that the family moves away to a different school district, forcing the child to integrate into an English-only program in the new location. Though family moves can occur at any point in a child's education, the natural break between elementary and secondary school is a time that some families opt for changes in location that they had avoided during the elementary school years.

A large number of immersion students choose to stay in the program and continue their language education in the secondary schools. Of those students I surveyed, nearly 86% remained in immersion classes in middle school, with slightly fewer, 80%, remaining for at least part of their high school years. Simon (1988) notes that students who studied foreign language in grade school are more likely than their peers to take a language in high school. He also cites a study at Harvard showing that college students who had studied a foreign language in elementary school were distinctly superior in foreign language skills than their peers at graduation from college. Sticking it out and putting in the time through high school pays rewards later on, both in competence and getting ahead in college.

You and your child have put a lot of effort into this program up to this point. Your child has mastered the school curriculum up until now. In this respect, nothing has changed. It may be time for you to give an additional little push to your child and also work as your child's advocate in finding solutions to any blocks in their path so that they can continue to completion of the immersion sequence.

Those students who choose to continue with language study are increasing the return on the investment their parents made when they entered kindergarten. Like any investment, the initial deposit remains, even without further deposits. But if one continues to reinvest and add additional resources, the net growth can be enormous.

> *"Middle school was actually easier. They became more confident in their learning. High school was even better. I didn't really have any concerns such as them being 'behind' as I knew they were still learning, only in a foreign language. No surprises, expected successes, and I am highly satisfied. I don't have any disappointments."*
> *– Lisa H, Language Immersion Parent*

The fact is that language learning takes time. A student who begins in high school can never catch up to a student who began in kindergarten, particularly if that early learner continues with language study through the K-12 experience. Language scholar James Asher notes:

> By the age of six a child has listened to his native language for 17,520 hours . . . In comparison, the student in the (traditional) classroom has listened to a foreign language for 320 hours . . . If we expect the (traditional college) student to have the fluency of a six-year-old child, the student should listen to the foreign language for 55 years of college instruction. (Asher in Simon 1988)

You can see that if an elementary language immersion experience provides up to 7,500 hours of target language exposure by fifth grade, continued study in middle and high school would be beneficial in reaching even higher levels of competency.

In Malcolm Gladwell's book, *Outliers*, he discusses the concept of "the 10,000 hour rule," or the time it takes to reach a high level of expertise at any skill (2008). Gladwell's work is based on that of Ericsson and colleagues (1993, 2007) in which it is noted that the development of expertise is related to how much time one spends developing those skills. This team of researchers posed that it would most likely take a minimum of ten years or 10,000 hours to develop high levels of expertise in any given skill area. Students in a K-12 experience may spend approximately 10,000 hours on their *entire* school experience. Eaton (2012) applied this 10,000-hour concept to language learning. Assuming that a student may receive 95 hours of language instruction per year in a typical high school class, it would take over 105 years to achieve expert levels of proficiency. If a student receives a total immersion experience of 7 hours per day, or approximately 1260 hours per year, it would take nearly 8 years to achieve an expert level of proficiency. And finally, if a student was in an immersion program for an entire K-12 experience, or 13 years, they could reach 10,000 hours with an average of slightly over 4 hours in language instruction per day. This is completely achievable, particularly if those hours are weighted toward the early elementary years. However, it remains necessary to continue with the language learning experience for many years to reach a high level of fluency.

Stephen Krashen, creator of the Monitor Model discussed in Chapter 1, has also studied the "critical age" of language learning. His extensive research on language learning supports the idea that *continuous* language learning is the key to delaying the end of the early critical time when the brain easily makes connections and pathways for language acquisition. He proposes that the "critical age" differs for different aspects of linguistic skill. For example, speech performance and pronunciation development are enhanced at an early age but the skills needed for abstract parts of language learning such as the semantics and syntax of language production continue into adolescence (Krashen 1981). This once again makes the argument for long-term language study and utilizing the middle and high school years for fine-tuning language skills, particularly in the production areas of speaking and writing.

> *"Middle school immersion students are over the language, but in high school they start to reap the benefits and many students go on to learn another language or study more Spanish. Almost all students are grateful at the end of high school for this gift. You are the parent. Push them to continue."* – Language Immersion Educator

> *"I'm always trying to improve my Spanish, but I am happy with my fluency. I use it to speak to my in-laws and I use it confidently in a professional setting."* – Maria C, Former Language Immersion Student

> *"I have translated a medical paper from English to Spanish, have interpreted in medical and dental clinics both ways, and also on a tour. The only way I think I could become more proficient is by living in a Spanish speaking country for an extended amount of time."* – Hannah C, Former Language Immersion Student

Value From Any Extended Language Experience

Whether your family stays with immersion education or makes the decision to leave the program, you can be assured that the time your child spent in immersion in the elementary years will not have been wasted. The student will draw upon that experience time and again in other coursework studied. The "gift" of immersion, a gift you provided as a parent, is always there as a resource and does not disappear.

"Overall best decision we ever made! Both kids have a better awareness of other worldviews and appreciate that they can communicate in two languages. They both excel in all other academics and how much of that is related to immersion would be hard to determine. They take on more academic challenges than I think they would have done had they not had to learn how to learn in a new language first." – Language Immersion Parent

Our own family moved away from our connection with a wonderful immersion program in Minnesota to Michigan, where our new district did not have an immersion program. One of my sons went into an English-only seventh grade class and the other into an English-only third grade classroom. As parents, we had to work to ensure their success. Our younger son came home in tears many nights, complaining of being bored. We solved this by keeping close contact with the school and providing lots of enrichment at home, as well as trips to museums and visits to other stimulating sites in the area. Each year became easier as we continued to advocate for our son until he reached the age where he was able to advocate for himself. We were fortunate that the school district was willing to work with us to provide opportunities for our son in middle school and high school to challenge him within the regular language program, AP courses, and dual enrollment.

My other son, having moved between sixth and seventh grades, transitioned easily and was excited by all the new opportunities in his new school, though they did not include language study. He had excellent Spanish skills after seven years in K-6 language immersion. Middle school beginning Spanish would not have been good for him, his teacher or the other students. Instead, once in high school, he took Spanish III and IV, passed the AP test, and then enrolled in college-level Spanish courses at a local college. Though it took advocacy on our part as parents, we were able to work with the district to find accommodations within the offerings they already had in place.

I know of several other language immersion parents who have advocated in this same manner, finding similar opportunities for their children. You must be willing to invest time to learn about options available, both within the local school district and with other academic institutions as well. Meet with administrators or counselors, prepared with options, suggestions and questions. Be prepared to listen to the constraints they have as well. Then, work together to find a solution that works for everyone.

What is interesting is that both our sons had different amounts of elementary immersion schooling. One had a two-year gap and one a four-year gap, yet both passed the AP test with ease. Both boys required the refinement of grammatical structures and struggled with using accent marks in their writing, but both had the skills needed to do well on the AP tests. They both claimed that the ability to listen to spoken Spanish without "freaking out" was the most valuable skill they applied to the testing process, and they gave language immersion learning the credit for their success on the exams. Advanced Placement credits also translate into real savings of time and dollars in college, something we appreciated as we started paying tuition bills. I share this experience because it reflects that of many families who have to move away during the 13 years their children are in elementary and secondary education. It also exemplifies the benefits of even limited years in an immersion program.

If you need to leave the program, be aware that you may need to provide extra stimulation for your child. Former immersion students have commented, "It's just too easy. They just tell you everything in English!" One student who moved away came back to visit me and said, "They don't learn anything in my new school. They just talk about stuff in English." It's interesting how immersion students grow to accept learning in another language as ordinary. They really do take it for granted and make the assumption that "school" means learning in a second language. As parents we forget they have never known education to be any other way.

THE LANGUAGE IMMERSION LIFE

If at some point you do have to leave your immersion program, it remains a valuable gift you have given your child. Even students who stayed in the program for only one or two years reported that the experience helped them do better than their peers in their high school language classes years later. Others report that it has helped them beyond formal education, as a lasting positive influence.

> *"I had only 3 years of immersion before I left the program and those 3 years of Spanish have landed me several jobs over the years where my Spanish skills were the deciding factor in my resume being taken out of the pile." – Erik M, Language Immersion Student, K-2nd grade*

> *"I went on to a middle and high school that was not equipped to continue my Spanish education. I am not as confident as I would like to be. However, when I am immersed back into it—I have retained most of it." – Annie P, Language Immersion Student, K-5th grade*

> *"I moved out of the immersion program at the end of 4th grade. I would have liked to continue with the program to reach higher levels of proficiency in Spanish, but I believe a good foundation was set. I have continued to learn and develop my Spanish as an adult, and I continue to progress. I have consistently heard that I make few errors and that my accent is good and understandable." – Allison M, Language Immersion Student, K-4th grade*

The benefits of language immersion, even for short periods of time, pay dividends for life. For example, even though my older son had seven years of immersion, he did not take any Spanish courses after graduating from high school. Several years later, in law school, he took a summer job at a law firm in Santiago, Chile.

where all of his work duties were in Spanish. After studying legal vocabulary, he was able to carry out his duties as if he had never stopped studying the language. Another interesting note is that two of the three short-term immersion students quoted above went on to become language immersion teachers themselves.

Continuing through the K-12 language learning experience, in whatever form that may take, is definitely a benefit to your child in attaining polished, educated skill in the language. However, do not let doubts about continuity or transition keep you from engaging in this wonderful educational opportunity, even for a short period of time. Whatever you can offer your child will be of value throughout their education and life beyond.

CHAPTER 9
The Language Immersion Afterlife

"My current life would simply not exist if I had not been an immersion student. It has affected my career, who I was able to marry, the language I speak with my son, where I travel to, where I shop, and so much more." – Katie Jo J-B, Language Immersion Student

I have been fortunate to have the acquaintance of thousands of former students, their parents, and numerous immersion educators who have left an imprint on me in so many ways. Their stories form the backdrop for the information I present here. Their experiences have inspired me to pass this knowledge on to future generations of immersion learners and their families. I believe so strongly in this form of education! These contacts form the voice that reaffirms those beliefs each year.

A great source of joy for me is learning of the successes of immersion students after they leave the K-12 sequence. The stories of success both in post-secondary education and in employment are overwhelming. Stories of love and family that emerge from the immersion experience are also fun to hear. I treasure the opportunities I have had to survey graduates of immersion programs and to talk with them personally on occasion. I am never disappointed in the stories I hear. The confidence and verbal abilities of immersion graduates contribute to the wealth of information they are willing to share.

> "I'm a completely different person than I would have been otherwise. I can confidently say that most of the opportunities I've had in my life were because of my immersion education. Yes, I learned a language, but it also really opens up the world to you. When you don't have that language barrier between you and a person or place, it seems so much more accessible!" – Talley S, Former Language Immersion Student

Post-Secondary Education

When immersion graduates were asked if they had attended college, nearly all responded affirmatively. Over half of those who attended college either majored or minored in their immersion program target language. Several students majored in language or culturally-related fields, and many combined their language major with another major in an entirely different field of study. Often students decided to major or minor in the language because they received so many AP, dual enrollment or placement test credits that it just made sense. Nearly 70% of immersion graduates received college credits for the language work they completed in high school, some even receiving enough credits to enter college with a language minor already completed. Why not include these credits on one's transcript in the form of a language major or minor? Why not graduate with this additional job skill added to one's résumé?

> "The Spanish major wasn't her love for the longest time, but now it is! She gets the gift!! Wow, only took us 20 years. Mom and Dad aren't always crazy. This was the right thing to do!" – Language Immersion Parent

Many immersion graduates have emphasized that they wanted to study a field that would allow them either to travel or to work with people from various cultures. After the language major, the most frequently listed major by former immersion students was International Business. It is interesting to note that the cultural aspects of immersion study seem to have as great an impact in later years as the language itself. One can also see that immersion graduates, like those of an English-only program, have a wide variety of interests that lead them in many different directions. In fact, the students who graduated from Spanish immersion programs listed the following majors in college:

Spanish (57%) as well as Culinary Arts, Management, **International Business, English**, Sociology, Secondary Education, Math, Psychology, Elementary Education, Finance, Marketing, Fine Arts, Electrical Engineering, Business, **Portuguese, Ethnic Studies, Global Studies,** Music Education, Mechanical Engineering, **English as a Second Language**, Physics, Microbiological Engineering, Communications, Economics, Pharmacy, Accounting, **Latin American Studies, International Relations, Italian, Arabic**, Biomedical Engineering, Chemical Engineering, Political Science, Philosophy, Nursing, Neuroscience, Graphic Design, Computer Science, Sociology, Art, Architecture, Theology, Religious Studies, Speech-Language Pathology, Pre-Physicians Assistant, Philosophy, Biology, Environmental Science, Chemistry, Communications, Photography, History, Agriculture, Child Development, Movement Therapy, Telecommunications, Journalism, Anthropology, Pre-Veterinary Medicine, Journalism, Construction, **Linguistics, French, Asian Studies**

- *Language, cultural and global related studies highlighted* (Mellgren and Somers 2008)

Travel

Parents should gain an early awareness that immersion students have a great interest in travel and study in other countries. This is not surprising, given that global awareness and cultural study is a focus of immersion programs. Over 70% of the graduates surveyed have indicated that they have traveled, studied or lived abroad.

> *"I lived abroad for about six years (Spain, France, Japan, Luxembourg, China and England.) I have traveled extensively. This passion came from the language Immersion Program." – Former Language Immersion Student*

> *"I definitely think I would be a different person had I gone to an English School. My Spanish made me want to travel. I have the lifelong dream of living in a third world Spanish speaking country providing medical services for a year. I know without a doubt, without my Spanish, I would not have that dream. I also think the cultural and global awareness is a huge aspect as well as learning to become independent which I didn't notice much until I was in college." – Hannah C, Former Language Immersion Student*

At the end of his first grade year my first child told me, "Mom, you might as well start getting used to it. I plan to go to the University of Tokyo when I graduate from high school." He actually ended up going to the University of Michigan, but still has a great interest in travel abroad and continues to do so with regularity. As a parent, it might be wise to prepare for the independence your child will surely develop and not be surprised when they inform you of their plans to study, live or travel extensively abroad.

"My daughter went on the Spanish Exchange trip in 8th grade and came home to tell me, "I'm totally independent now. All I need is food and laundry." We laughed because, of course, she also cooks for herself and does her own laundry. After walking with groups of friends through the streets of Madrid, getting around on her own felt like nothing." – Lisa M, Language Immersion Parent

You want a globally aware, independent child? You will certainly get one with an immersion student! Some parents have fears that this type of education will cause them to lose their kids to the world, that they will choose to live in a faraway land. This is a valid concern. It could happen! Be prepared that this is a risk you are taking, one that can be positive or negative, depending on your own comfort level with high levels of independence in your child.

I find that of the thousands of immersion students I have known, this openness to differing cultures is nearly universal. That interest and craving to explore the world is fostered from that very first day of kindergarten when the student comes face to face with another language, the very basis of culture.

"To develop real understanding of another culture requires us to experience that culture in context, rather than simply memorizing facts or imitating stereotypes. Cross-cultural competency also means being able to live in different cultures and move across different societies fluently. In the globalized world, it is impossible to be competent in all world cultures, but it is essential to be open to new and different cultures. Proficiency in foreign languages is essential." (Zhao, 2009b)

The exposure that results from time in an immersion program fosters not only interest and understanding, but also *competency* to live, study, and work in different cultures successfully. So, if your child decides to spend a period of time in another cultural setting, whether near or far, you can be confident that they have developed a skill level that helps them function well. They will have a fabulous time and will come home (most do decide to return home) an enriched individual.

When asked about study-abroad programs in college, over 60% of immersion students either had studied abroad or had plans to do so. Of those who studied abroad, over 90% chose to study in a country where the language learned through immersion is spoken.

"I did a semester study abroad in college. It was a wonderful experience and with my strong language background I was able to actually enroll in typical courses, with native Spaniards rather than take Spanish language classes with other exchange students, which in my opinion provided a much more authentic experience."
– Former Language Immersion Student

In surveying former Spanish immersion students I found that virtually every country where the target language is spoken had students who have lived, studied or traveled there. Many graduates have done this repeatedly, through multiple visits to countries where they speak the language. Many have extended their experiences abroad for years, and many are still living in settings where they speak the language of their new environment fluently. Other students are living in countries, not where their second language is spoken, but where they are simply receiving another cross cultural-experience—acting on those values instilled while studying in the immersion program. In fact, quite a few of the responses to my surveys arrived from sites all over the globe where these immersion graduates were studying, living, and working.

Employment Opportunities

"I have put it to use at every job I've held." – Former Language Immersion Student

Immersion graduates indicate that they have had multiple opportunities to use their language skills in a work setting. In fact, fewer than 8% of students surveyed indicated that they were not aware of using their language skills in their employment. The vast majority has experienced opportunities to speak the target language with customers and co-workers, as teachers with students or parents, or working in sales, customer service, marketing, mission work, tutoring, and translation. It is immensely satisfying to read comments about how many graduates use their language skills every day. Many employers rely upon these employees to translate on a regular basis. The experiences and stories shared here are the results of my own surveys of students from Spanish immersion programs. It is possible that the use of other languages in the workplace may not be quite as prevalent as the use of Spanish, but I am convinced opportunities exist in other languages as well in our diverse country.

Many former students have indicated that they not only utilize the language, but also actually obtained their current positions due to the fact that they could speak a second language. While not all are employed in positions where the language is used as part of their job duties, the fact that they *had* the language skills influenced hiring decisions. Others note that the influence of the immersion experience allowed them to be more successful at arriving at their current choice of employment.

"My ability to speak Spanish got me in the door." – Former Language Immersion Student

"Every single job I've had since I was 18 has involved Spanish. I worked in a call center answering Spanish calls, at the university teaching Spanish conversation classes, as an interpreter, and now as a full-time translator. I wouldn't be the same person if I hadn't gone through the immersion program." – Former Language Immersion Student

"I think that having the ability to communicate with others when it is not expected is so much more valuable and rewarding. I coach a collegiate sports team and many of my students grew up speaking languages other than English. Having learned another language at an early age, I have developed more empathy and understanding for language barriers and nuanced speech/writing of those who are communicating in English as their second (or third) language. [Language Immersion] was such a wonderful opportunity for me and continues to prove its value regularly." – Former Language Immersion Student

"I now live permanently in Spain and have my own freelance translation business. I'm often confused for a native speaker. Lots of people can't believe I'm from Minnesota! I don't know any other native English speaker living here who speaks as well as I do. I have the immersion program to thank for that." – Former Language Immersion Student

"My Spanish has truly given me a direction in life I could have never imagined. I've coordinated a medical clinic in the Dominican Republic, experienced the Dominican cultures and made lifelong cross-cultural relationships. One of the proudest compliments I have ever received is a Dominican telling me he didn't know I was American. He guessed I was from Spain based on my accent."
– Former Language Immersion Student

Lifetime Language Skills

"I love knowing a second language and it always amazes others when they find out I can speak fluently." – Language Immersion Student

In rating their own language skills, most immersion graduates still feel they have an adequate use of the language, even though many have not taken a formal class in several years, and some for over 15 years. A full 65% of surveyed graduates claim fluency in reading, listening, speaking and writing in the second language, while 28% claim to understand most of the language they hear and say they have retained a basic vocabulary in the language. Only 7% claimed a lesser understanding but still believe they have basic skills.

Many former immersion students note that they also use their language skills for volunteer work, simply to help out interpreting at stores, restaurants, and medical appointments, or for communication with neighbors and colleagues. Several have become Peace Corp, AmeriCorps, medical and mission trip volunteers; teachers or interpreters for social service organizations such as health clinics, food banks and shelters; campaign and other political volunteers; and either exchange students themselves or hosts of foreign exchange students. All of these volunteer opportunities allowed them the occasion to practice and maintain their immersion language. This returns us to the social and interpersonal skills discussed in Chapter 2. Using the language in one's daily life on a regular basis is a significant outgrowth of the program, and many immersion graduates confirm that this is an important benefit of the program, which has a major impact on their current lifestyles.

"I use my Spanish every day communicating with customers, co-workers and a few of the wonderful people I volunteer with. My

immersion friends and I use it as a secret language around non-Spanish speakers too! Its a huge part of my life, and I'm so grateful for it." – Former Language Immersion Student

"To this day, I'm in touch with other kids from my immersion class and all of our careers were shaped by our time in immersion, most of us using our language professionally in some way." – Ellen T, Former Language Immersion Student

Overall Impact of Immersion Education

In *A Rationale For Foreign Language Education, A Position Paper of the National Council of State Supervisors of Foreign Languages (NCSSFL),* educators from across the country summarize the value of language learning:

> Perhaps the broadest and most important function of all foreign language study is to provide a more liberating educational experience for students—the vocationally oriented as well as the college bound, the poor, as well as the middle-class and the rich. As students are given the opportunity to learn a foreign language, they have the unique opportunity to understand the nature of themselves as young men and women and their relationship to the world about them, benefits which all of our students will need and will carry with them far beyond the language classroom. (2004)

While this statement is made for all language learning, we know that developing competence at a high level takes years, something that is more likely to be achievable in a language immersion program. Students also gain the many other positive benefits that have been reviewed and discussed here. Indeed, the impact of this experience is enormous as has been observed by researchers, administrators, teachers, parents, and the students themselves.

In response to two different questions, 91% of former students felt that language immersion had been *valuable* in their life experience. A full 97% of students surveyed believe that language immersion has had an *overall positive impact* on their lives. Whether proclaiming immersion to be *valuable,* or to have *positive impact,* graduates have a full sense of satisfaction with the immersion experience. They certainly appear to recognize the value of learning a second language from childhood. Several former students already have their own children enrolled in immersion programs, having learned firsthand the value of learning a language as a child. Others proclaim, "I hope to place my child in an immersion program!" or "I am a huge advocate of immersion education for any child!" When asked, "If you could do it over, would you still hope your parents would place you in an immersion program?" every single immersion graduate answered yes, they would do immersion again.

"I absolutely would do it again, and in the future would send my kids through the program as well. Academically it challenged me and made me a better person." – Morgan P, Former Language Immersion Student

"Best thing my parents ever did for me. Hands down." – Sally H C, Former Language Immersion Student

"I loved my education so much growing up in an immersion setting that I never wanted to leave. My goal was to one day go back there, as a classroom teacher. I was hired as a Spanish immersion teacher back at the elementary school where I attended. I am forever grateful for my immersion experience." – Former Language Immersion Student

> *"I am proud to say I am bilingual and have no fear of traveling to any Spanish speaking country. I have had more opportunities in high school and college because of my Spanish experience. Even though there were challenges, I'm glad my parents put me through it." – Former Language Immersion Student*

Young adults who are products of immersion programs are confident, successful and full of hopes and dreams for changing the world. Many have studied Spanish for nearly 20 years or more and are shining examples of the bonuses of immersion education. These former students stated:

- My life would be completely different without immersion.
- I believe [language immersion] really opens the eyes of students at an early age and helps them in our globalizing world.
- The value contributed to my life has not come in the way of just the use of Spanish, but also in the early development changes that the program instilled in my brain during immersion education.
- Putting me in language immersion was one of the best things my parents ever did for me!
- My years in the language immersion program continue to positively impact me. I will always regard the experience as one of the most beneficial of my life.
- Language immersion is one of the best things that have ever happened to me! It has had more of an influence on my life than my parents could've ever imagined.
- Language immersion is the reason for my Spanish proficiency, and hence, my passions and career goals!
- It has affected everything I do and everything that I want to do. It is so beneficial to be able to understand and relate to other cultures. It makes you more open minded and more

able to interact with different kinds of people. We have all been given an amazing gift that will help us be successful all throughout our lives.
- When I was little I assumed everyone learned to read Spanish before they learned to read English. It wasn't until much later that I learned we were an elite few.

(Mellgren and Somers, 2008)

It is truly an amazing legacy that immersion education bestows on students. As one of our graduates stated, "Our parents thought it was about the language. I'm here to tell you it's not about the language but rather the acceptance and understanding of other cultures. That is what has made the biggest impact on my life" (Cisneros 2007). Another student adds, "An immersion school prepares you academically for life. You become a constant learner." These are people who accept and understand others and are changing the planet through their contacts with friends, colleagues, neighbors and children. I, for one, am proud to know them all, and continue to watch for the great things they are accomplishing.

Curtain and Pesola (1988) noted in their work with immersion programs that children only achieve the full potential of their extended experience in language learning when they also achieve a measure of competence in the areas of culture, empathy for other people, and global awareness. Elementary language learning may be the best way to teach the next generation not to discriminate against or be intolerant of people simply because they are culturally different (Lipton 1998).

"I got the same education the non-immersion kids did, plus a cultural education that I would pay millions for again." – Talley S, Former Language Immersion Student

> *"Language learning is a gift you give to your child. It cannot be taken away. Don't let your own fears or insecurities prevent you from giving this opportunity to your child. Many, many doors will be opened for them."* – Mary Jeanne S, Language Immersion Teacher and Parent

Children cannot choose this opportunity for themselves. Only parents can take the step to offer the world of languages to their children. Your child depends on you to make wise decisions that will prove beneficial years from now. I love this short essay, written by a first grade student with his newly developing language skills, about his parents:

Mis Padres
Mis padres son los mejores padres en el mundo porque hace cosas que yo no necesita este es porque son los mejores padres y los amo muchisimo pero hace errors como todos los padres y como los chicos tambien y este es porque los amo mucho.

My Parents (translation)
My parents are the best parents in the world because (they) do things I don't need this is why they are the best parents and I love them so much but (they) make mistakes like all parents and like children too and this is why I love them a lot.

Perfect? Of course not. Grammatically correct? Like all first graders, not yet. Understandable by his native speaking teacher? Absolutely. This six-year-old student is able to express himself in another language, to a native speaker, with emotion that is communicated clearly. As a parent, do you want that? Oh, I hope I have convinced you that you absolutely will want this opportunity for your child.

As we look at immersion education and review the data available about the academic success of immersion students, there are abundant reasons to consider this choice for your child and your family. However, as language immersion graduates indicate in such a unified voice, the real gifts of immersion education reach far beyond academic success. Immersion education develops the kind of global graduate we need in our changing world. The immediate success is obvious; the immersion lifestyle is forever.

Acknowledgements

Many immersion colleagues, who are also immersion parents, could have written this book. However these warriors of early language learning are busy preparing lessons everyday, in all subjects, in a foreign language, or in two languages. To every immersion teacher and administrator I offer my gratitude and respect for the energy and passion you bring to work each day. In particular, I wish to thank those I worked with at the Robbinsdale Spanish Immersion School, and the Ada Vista Spanish Immersion School. Your dedication, support and friendship made every day a true pleasure. You have always been, and continue to be, the inspiration for my ongoing passion for immersion education.

Thank you to the hundreds of students, parents and educators who answered my surveys. You gave of your time and energy to contribute to this project and I am grateful beyond measure. Many of your responses brought back great memories, causing me to smile and even laugh out loud at the recollections you shared. To the students in particular, I appreciate the updates I received on your successes in life. I am so proud of each and every one of you for the contributions you continue to make on our planet.

I am in great debt to Ann Olberg Millán, Diane Geisen Angelo, Kathleen Pool, Emily Pool, Laura Macartney, Sue Gutierrez, Carol

Ann Dahlberg, John Mellgren, Erik Mellgren and Jeff Mellgren for reading various drafts and providing genuinely helpful comments and suggestions. The gift of your time to read the manuscript with your teacher pens out is cherished, as well as your ongoing friendship and support.

My tremendous editor, Lisa McNeilley, not only encouraged me but also championed the book from the start. Thank you for your guidance, your frankness, and your caring for the message itself. As a language immersion parent, the insight and professionalism you brought to the editing process was unique. I treasure your extraordinary contributions.

Kathy Boyce, my high school English teacher, not only demanded the writing and re-writing of multiple drafts my senior year, but more importantly introduced me to *For Whom the Bell Tolls*. Thank you for the gift of Ernest Hemingway, who is still my favorite author. Ms. Boyce, you remain my most influential writing teacher, and I am grateful for the red ink marks and suggestions offered so freely years ago.

To all the *Hermanas de Albeniz*, you have encouraged me beyond belief. I am so grateful for your friendship and sharing of adventure in both life and languages. You have been my supportive sisters for 30 years, since our summer in the *sartén* of Madrid. *Polvos son.*

My parents, Gilbert and Lois Park, taught by example how to lead in education. Mom always knew I should be in an elementary school, long before I knew it myself. She was a great teacher and modeled the many hours of dedication needed to do it well. Dad was my first elementary school principal and from him I learned how to be a great administrator. He also taught me that spelling is important and constantly encouraged creativity in my writing. Thank you both for making sure I learned the importance of music, dancing, and art in addition to academics.

My sons, John and Erik, as young boys spent countless hours waiting in my classroom after school as I prepared lessons, changed bulletin boards, organized folders and engaged in many other acts of immersion teaching. Thank you for your tolerance and independence. You are fine young men, making great contributions to the world. I couldn't be prouder of you both. Language immersion has served you well and I am happy to have witnessed your growth and success in two languages. Thank you for being the source of so many stories in this book.

And to Jeff, who stayed home alone with a 5-year-old and a 1-year-old for an entire summer so I could start the adventure that opened the door to my own path in language immersion, thank you. You know this field intimately having lived in an immersion family for the past 30 years as well. Your support as I explored new opportunities has been unwavering. I always knew I would be able to attempt the next thing that intrigued me. You know as well as anyone—the language immersion life lasts forever—and it's a pretty good life.

Resources

The Center for Advanced Research on Language Acquisition (CARLA)
http://carla.umn.edu/immersion/index.html
CARLA is a significant resource for practitioners, researchers and others interested in learning more about immersion education, and serves as one of the U.S. Department of Education's Title VI National Language Resource Centers. CARLA supports immersion education through providing a network dedicated to exchanging information, research findings, and resources. It offers professional development for educators through the Summer Institutes program. CARLA also hosts the Immersion and Dual Language Education Conference each year and maintains archives of videos, handouts and other presentation documents on their website. In addition, there are links to research briefs, bibliographies, directories, FAQs and numerous other resources of interest to educators, researchers, and parents interested in immersion education.

American Council on Immersion Education (ACIE)
http://carla.umn.edu/immersion/acie.html
The **ACIE** served as an organizational network for those interested in immersion education from 1997-2011. It was housed at CARLA at the University of Minnesota and published the *ACIE Newsletter*, an important publication and resource. Unfortunately, funding cuts forced the suspension of this significant newsletter but you can still find archives of articles from past issues on the CARLA website found above.

The Center for Applied Linguistics (CAL)
http://www.cal.org/
CAL is located in Washington DC and is known for its work in bilingual and dual language education, English as a second language education, world language education and many other projects in language learning and cultural understanding. CAL provides many resources including research, policy information, training and other services to language programs. They maintain a directory on immersion and other dual language and bilingual programs that can be found at the following link: http://www.cal.org/resource-center/databases-directories.

Language Resource Centers (LRCs)
http://www.nflrc.org/lrcs.php
There are sixteen LRCs located at universities across the United States created by the Department of Education to provide expertise, conduct research, and offer resources and professional development in language learning. Some centers concentrate on specific language areas and others on foreign languages in general. There are links to each of the sixteen sites on the main LRC web page.

National Network for Early Language Learning (NNELL)
https://nnell.org/
NNELL provides a network to support early language teaching and learning. Focused on K-8 education, NNELL is a resource for educators, parents and policymakers. The organization is committed to promote opportunities for all children to develop a high level of competence in at least one language and culture in addition to their own. The NELL website has links for parents and educators filled with information about events, webinars, newsletters, journals and other resources in early language learning.

References

American Academy of Arts and Sciences. 2017. *America's Languages: Investing in Language Education for the 21st Century*. Commission on Language Learning. https://www.amacad.org/language.

American Councils for International Education. 2016. Why the Dual Language Immersion Approach Will Change Achievement in American Public Schools. (May 4th). http://americancouncils.org/news/why-dual-language-immersion-approach-will-change-achievement-american-public-schools.

Au-Yeung, Karen, Kathleen Hipfner-Boucher, I Chen, Adrian Pasquarella, Nadia D'Angelo, and S. Hélène Deacon. 2015. Development of English and French Language and Literacy Skills in EL1 and EL French Immersion Students in the Early Grades. *Reading Research Quarterly* 50 (2) 233-254. ERIC Number EJ1055945.

Barr-Harrison, Pat. 2003. High School Immersion in the United States: A Research Study. *The ACIE Newsletter* 6 (3) 10, 11, 16.

Bhattacharjee, Yudhijit. 2012. Why Bilinguals Are Smarter. *The New York Times* (March 17). http://www.nytimes.com/2012/03/18/opinion/sunday/the-benefits-of-bilingualism.html.

Bialystok, Ellen Kathleen F. Peets, and Sylvain Moreno. 2014. Producing Bilinguals Through Immersion Education: Development of Metalinguistic Awareness. *Applied Psycholinguistics* 35 (1) 177-191. ERIC Number EJ1016163

Blonigan, Maria. 2001. Insights from an Immersion Survivor. *The ACIE Newsletter* 5 (1) 11.

Burnett, Wendy J. 1990. The Hidden Handicap: French Immersion and Children with Learning Disabilities. *So You Want Your Child to Learn French?* 2d ed. Ottawa, Canada: Canadian Parents for French.

Bruck, Margaret. 1978. The Suitability of Early French Immersion Programs for the Language-Disabled Child. *Canadian Journal of Education* 3 (4) 51-72. DOI: 10.2307/1494685.

———. 1985. Consequences of Transfer Out of Early French Immersion Programs. *Applied Psycholinguistics* 6 (2) 101-120. DOI:10.1017/S0142716400006068

Boudreaux, Nicole. 2011. Exploring French Immersion Student Attrition in Louisiana: Who Leaves, When, and Why? *The ACIE Newsletter* 14 (2) 1, 4-8.

Campbell, Russell N. 1984. The Immersion Approach to Foreign Language Teaching. In *Studies on Immersion Education.* California State Department of Education.

Carver-Akers, Kateri. 2013. Building Intercultural Competency in the Language Immersion Montessori Classroom. *Learning Languages* (Spring/Summer) 38-42.

Center for Applied Linguistics. 2011. *Directory of Foreign Language Immersion Programs in U.S. Schools.* http://www.cal.org/resource-center/databases-directories.

Central Intelligence Agency. 2010. CIA Director Calls for a National Commitment to Language Proficiency at Foreign Language Summit. *Central Intelligence Agency News and Information* (December 8). https://www.cia.gov/news-information/press-releases-statements/press-release-2010/foreign-language-summit.html

Chrapek, Greg. 2016. *Sportsmanship and Academics Shine Through in Baseball Game* (April 28). Grand Rapids, MI: Advance Newspapers.

Cisneros, Maria Blonigan. 2007. Statement given at the 20th Anniversary Celebration of the Robbinsdale Immersion Program in Robbinsdale, Minnesota.

Colletta, S.P., Clement, R. and Edwards, H.P. 1983. *Community and Parental Influence: Effects on Student Motivation and French Second Language Proficiency.* Quebec, Canada: International Center for Research on Bilingualism.

Cummins, Jim. 2000. Immersion Education for the Millennium: What We Have Learned from 30 Years of Research on Second Language Immersion. https://www.researchgate.net/publication/255638397_Immersion_Education_for_the_Millennium_What_We_Have_Learned_from_30_Years_of_Research_on_Second_Language_Immersion.

Curtain, Helena Anderson and Carol Ann Pesola. 1988. *Languages and Children— Making the Match.* Reading, MA: Addison-Wesley Publishing Company.

Curtain, Helena and Carol Ann Dahlberg. 2010. *Languages and Children—Making the Match*, 4th ed. Boston: Pearson.

Cusido, Carmen. 2017. Report: Want the Job? Be Able to Say So in More than One Language. NBC News (March 13). http://www.nbcnews.com/news/latino/report-want-job-be-able-say-so-more-one-language-n732486.

Downs-Reid, David. 2000. Using English Achievement Data to Promote Immersion Education. *The ACIE Newsletter* 3 (March).

Eaton, Sarah Elaine. 2012. How Will Alberta's Second Language Students Ever Achieve Proficiency? The ACTFL Proficiency Guidelines, the CEFR and the "10,000-Hour Rule" in Relation to the Alberta K-12 Language-Learning Context. *Notos*, 12 (2) 2-12.

Ericsson, K. A., R. Krampe and C. Tesch-Römer. 1993. The Role of Deliberate Practice in the Acquisition of Expert Performance. *Psychological Review* 100, 363-406, cited in Eaton 2012.

Ericsson K.A., M.J. Prietula, and E.T. Cokely. 2007. The Making of an Expert. *Harvard Business Review* 85, 114-121, cited in Eaton 2012.

Feenstra, H. J. 1969. Parent and Teacher Attitudes: Their Role in Second-Language Acquisition. *Canadian Modern Language Review* 26, 5-13.

Fortune, Tara Williams. 2012. What the Research Says About Immersion. In *Chinese Language Learning in the Early Grades*. Asia Society, 9-13. http://asiasociety.org/education/chinese-language-initiatives/chinese-language-learning-early-grades.

Fortune, Tara Williams and Mandy Menke. 2009. Understanding Language and Learning Disabilities in Immersion Education: Immersion Educators' Top Questions and Research-Based, Practitioner-Informed Responses. *The ACIE Newsletter* 12 (2).

Friedman, Amelia. 2015. America's Lacking Language Skills. *The Atlantic* (May 10). https://www.theatlantic.com/education/archive/2015/05/filling-americas-language-education-potholes/392876/

Gaarder, Bruce. The Golden Rules of Second Language Acquisition by Young Children. *Journal for the National Association for Bilingual Education*, 2 (2): 59 (1978).

Gardner, R.C. 1968. Attitudes and Motivation: Their Role in Second-Language Acquisition. *TESOL Quarterly* 2, 141-150.

Genesee, Fred. 2012. The Suitability of Immersion for all Learners: What Does the Research Say? Presentation at the Center for Advanced Research in Language Acquisition (CARLA) Research Convocation. http://www.carla.umn.edu/conferences/past/immersion2012/handouts/Genesee_At-risklearners_PPT.pdf.

Gladwell, Malcolm. 2008. *Outliers: The Story of Success.* Boston: Little, Brown and Company.

Gouin, Donna. 2009. Review of Learning to Read in a Second Language, Presentation by Fred Genesee at October 2008 Pathways to Bilingualism and Beyond Conference. *The ACIE Newsletter* 12 (3) 8-11.

Hibbeln, Michael J. 2004. English Language and Math Achievement of Third Grade Spanish Immersion Students Compared to

Students in a Traditional English Only Program. Master's Thesis, Michigan State University.

Hillary, Wendy. 2007. Gains in Literacy Development through Second Language Immersion. Master's thesis. Western Michigan University.

Individuals with Disabilities Act of 2004. Washington D.C.: U.S. Department of Education. http://idea.ed.gov/explore/view/p/, root, regs, 300, A, 300.8,.html.

Jackson, Anthony W., Charles E. M. Kolb, and John I. Wilson. The National Imperative For Language Learning. *Education Week*, 30 (18): 25, 32 (2011).

Jerome, Sarah D. (2007). Leading Schools for Global Literacy. *The School Administrator*, 64 (9) 60.

Johnson, Martha. 2003. Organizational Pointers for Secondary Immersion Parents. *The ACIE Newsletter* 6 (3) 9.

Jones, Cordell T. 2005. Spanish Immersion and the Academic Success of Alamo Heights Students. *The ACIE Newsletter* 9 (1) 6-7, 14-15.

Joy, Rhonda. 2011. The Concurrent Development of Spelling Skills in Two Languages. *International Electronic Journal of Elementary Education* 3 (2) 105-121. ERIC Number: EJ1052394.

Kinzler, Katherine. 2016. The Superior Social Skills of Bilinguals. *The New York Times* (March 11). https://www.nytimes.com/2016/03/13/opinion/sunday/the-superior-social-skills-of-bilinguals.html.

Konyndyk, Irene Brouwer. 2011. *Foreign Languages for Everyone.* Grand Rapids, MI: Edenridge Press.

Krashen, Stephen D. 1981. Aptitude and Attitude in relation to Second Language Acquisition and Learning. In *Individual Differences and Universals in Language Learning Aptitude,* edited by Karl C. Diller. Rowley, MA: Newbury House Publishers, Inc.

———. 1984. Immersion: Why It Works and What It Has Taught Us. *Language and Society* 12, 61-64. Ottawa, Canada: Commissioner of Official Languages.

Kruk, Richard S., and Kristin A. A. Reynolds. 2012. French Immersion Experience and Reading Skill Development in At-Risk Readers. *Journal of Child Language* 39 (3) 580-610. ERIC number EJ971222.

Lambert, Wallace E. 1984. An Overview of Issues in Immersion Education. In *Studies on Immersion Education.* California State Department of Education.

Lambert, W.E. and J. MacNamara. 1969. Some Cognitive Consequences of Following a First-Grade Curriculum in a Second Language. *Journal of Educational Psychology* 60 (2): 86-96. http://dx.doi.org/10.1037/h0027092.

Lapkin, Sharon and James Cummins. 1984. Canadian French Immersion Education: Current Administrative and Instructional Practices. In *Studies on Immersion Education.* California State Department of Education.

Lindholm-Leary, Kathryn. 2011. Student Outcomes in Chinese Two-Way Immersion Programs: Language Proficiency, Academic Achievement and Student Attitudes. In *Immersion Education: Practices, Policies, Possibilities,* edited by Diane J. Tedick, Donna Christian and Tara Williams Fortune. Bristol: Multilingual Matters.

———. 2014. *Importance of Bilingualism on Student Outcomes: Focus on Grades Preschool – Third.* Presentation at Immersion 2014: Fifth International Conference on Language Immersion Education, Salt Lake City, UT. http://www.lindholm-leary.com/resources/Presentations/UtahImmersionResearch2014b.pdf.

———. 2015. *Student Outcomes in Dual Language Programs.* American Educational Research Association. http://www.lindholm-leary.com/resources/Presentations/2015AERA_Symp_KLL.pdf.

———. 2016a. Student's Perceptions of Bilingualism in Spanish and Mandarin Dual Language Programs. *International Multilingual Research Journal* 10 (1): 59-70. http://dx.doi.org/10.1080/19313152.2016.1118671.

———. 2016b. *The Transformative Power of Dual Language Programs.* Presentation at EL Alliance, March, Eugene, OR. http://www.lindholm-leary.com/resources/Presentations/Handout_ELAlliance2016_Keynote.pptx.pdf.

Lipton, Gladys C. 1998. *Elementary Foreign Language Programs.* Lincolnwood, IL: National Textbook Company.

Lipton, G., R. Morgan and M. Reed. 1996. Does FLES* Help AP French Students Perform Better? *ATTF National Bulletin* 21 (4) cited in Lipton, Gladys C. 1998.

Macartney, Laura. 2011. Reading Writing, and Immersion. Personal Newsletter.

McEldowney, Nancy. 2015. Fast Forward: US Diplomacy in an Untethered World. *World Affairs* (Summer). http://www.worldaffairsjournal.org/print/100434.

McGinn, Gail H. 2015. *Foreign Language, Cultural Diplomacy, and Global Security.* http://www.amacad.org/multimedia/pdfs/Foreign-Language-Cultural-Diplomacy-Global-Security.pdf.

Mellgren, Millie Park and Emily Somors. 2008. Graduates of a Language Immersion Program: What Are They Doing Now? *The ACIE Newsletter* 12 (1) 1-8.

Montanari, SImona, Gabriela Simón-Cereijido, and Antonella Hartel. 2016. The Development of Writing Skills in an Italian-English Two-Way Immersion Program: Evidence from First Through Fifth Grade. *International Multilingual Research Journal* 10 (1) 44-58. ERIC Number EJ1088024.

Montone, Christopher L., and Michael I. Loeb. 2003. Implementing Two-Way Immersion Programs in Secondary Schools. The *ACIE Newsletter* 6 (3) 1-8.

Myers, Marjorie L. 2011. Achievement of Children Identified with Special Needs in Two-Way Spanish/English Immersion Programs. The *ACIE Newsletter* 14 (2) 1-8.

National Council of State Supervisors of Foreign Languages (NCSSFL). 2004. A Rationale for Foreign Language Education. Position Paper.

Nelson, Sarah. 2006. From French Immersion Student to French Immersion teacher. The *ACIE Newsletter* 9 (2) 9.

Nicolay, Anne-Catherine and Martine Poncelet. 2012. Cognitive Advantage in Children Enrolled in a Second-Language Immersion Elementary School Program for Three Years. *Cambridge Core* 16 (3). https://doi.org/10.1017/S1366728912000375.

Nord, C., Roey, S., Perkins, R., Lyons, M., Lemanski, N., Brown, J., and Schuknecht, J. 2011. *The Nation's Report Card: America's High School Graduates.* NCES 2011, 462. U.S. Department of Education, National Center for Education Statistics. Washington DC: U.S. Government Printing Office.

Pesola, Carol Ann. 1988. Articulation for Elementary School Foreign Language Programs: Challenges and Opportunities. In *Shaping the Future of Foreign Language Education: FLES, Articulation, and Proficiency,* edited by John F. Lalande II. Lincolnwood, IL: National Textbook Company.

Pool, Kathleen J. 2003. Motivation and Language Inside and Outside of the Immersion Classroom. Master's Project Paper, Calvin College.

Pufahl, Ingrid and Nancy C. Rhodes. 2011. Foreign Language Instruction in U.S. Schools: Results of a National Survey of Elementary and Secondary Schools. *Foreign Language Annals* 44 (2, Summer), 258-288.

Saville-Troike, Muriel, Erica McClure and Mary Fritz. 1984. Communicative Tactics in Children's Second Language Acquisition. In *Universals of Second Language Acquisition,* edited by Fred R. Eckman, Lawrence H. Bell and Diane Nelson. Rowley, MA: Newbury House Publishers, Inc.

Schachter, Ron. 2011. Global Learning Scales Up. *District Administration* (March) 52-58.

Simon, Paul. 1988. *The Tongue-Tied American*. New York: Continuum Publishing Company.

Steele, Jennifer L., Robert Slater, Jennifer Li, Gema Zamarro, Trey Miller. 2013. The Effect of Dual-Language Immersion on Student Achievement in Math, Science, and English Language Arts. Society for Research on Educational Effectiveness Fall Conference. ERIC Number: ED564065

Swain, Merrill (1984). A Review of Immersion Education in Canada: Research and Evaluation Studies. In *Studies on Immersion Education*, Office of Bilingual Bicultural Education, California State Department of Education, 87-112.

Sykes, Julie M., Linda B. Forrest, and Kathryn J. Carpenter. 2016. Building a Successful and Sustainable Language Immersion Program: The Portland, Oregon, Mandarin Dual Language Experience, Parts I and II. Eugene, OR: Center for Applied Second Language Studies. http://casls.uoregon.edu/wp-content/uploads/sites/7/2016/11/Flagship-Ethnography-Part-I-Revised.pdf, http://casls.uoregon.edu/wp-content/uploads/sites/7/2016/11/Flagship-Ethnography-Part-II-Revised.pdf.

Tran, Natalie A., Sam Behseta, Mark Ellis, Armando Martinez-Cruz and Jacqueline Contreras. 2015. The Effects of Spanish English Dual Language Immersion on Student Achievement in Science and Mathematics. *eJournal of Education Policy* (Special Issue) 57-77. http://nau.edu/COE/eJournal.

Wall Street Journal. 2012. The Bilingual Brain is Sharper and More Focused, Study Says. (April 30). http://blogs.wsj.com/health/2012/04/30/the-bilingual-brain-is-sharper-and-more-focused-study-says/tab/print/.

Weise, Elizabeth. 2014. *A Parent's Guide to Mandarin Immersion*. San Francisco: Chenery Street Press.

Wilberschied, Lee. 2005. Fostering Philoxenia: Understanding and Integrating Culture. *The Year of Languages: Challenges, Changes and Choices*. Report of the Central States Conference on the Teaching of Foreign Languages, 15-23.

Wise, Nancy, and Xi Chen. 2010. At-Risk Readers in French Immersion: Early Identification and Early Intervention. *Canadian Journal of Applied Linguistics* 13 (2) 128-149. ERIC Number EJ944135.

Wise, Nancy, Nadia D'Angelo and Xi Chen. 2016. A School-Based Phonological Awareness Intervention for Struggling Readers in Early French Immersion. *Reading and Writing: An Interdisciplinary Journal* 29 (2) 183-205. ERIC Number EJ1089591.

Woelber, Kristine M-W. 2004. Underachieving Students and the Child Study Team: Determining Eligibility for Special Education Services. The *ACIE Newsletter* 7 (3) 6-7, 11-15.

WOODtv8. 2017. Jenison Parents Queue a Day Early for Spanish Immersion. (March 26) Grand Rapids, MI. http://

woodtv.com/2017/03/26/jenison-parents-queue-a-day-early-for-spanish-immersion/.

Yamauchi, Lois A., Jo-Anne Lau-Smith, and Rebecca J. I. Luning. 2008. Family Involvement in a Hawaiian Language Immersion Program. *The School Community Journal* 18 (1) 39-55.

Zachmeier-Ruh, Marcy, and Mary-Fred Bausman-Watkins. 2005. Twin Cities German Immersion School: Educating Children for Bilingual, Informed, and Active World Citizenship. *The ACIE Newsletter* 9 (1) 9, 12-13, 15.

Zhao, Yong. 2008. What Knowledge Has the Most Worth? *The School Administrator* 65 (2) 20-26.

———. 2009a. *Catching Up or Leading the Way*. Alexandria, VA: ASCD.

———. 2009b. Needed: Global Villagers. *Educational Leadership* 67 (1) 60-65.

Made in the USA
Middletown, DE
25 September 2019